QUINTESSENCE

QUINTESSENCE

THE QUALITY OF HAVING *IT*

by Betty Cornfeld & Owen Edwards

Book design by John C. Jay
Photographs by Dan Kozan

Crown Publishers, Inc., New York

Our thanks to Evelyn Roth
and Mary Kelly, whose energetic
and intelligent help was indispensable.
And to Pam Thomas, our editor, whose
guidance, patience, care,
and occasional feeding
kept entropy at bay.

Trademarked products mentioned in the book are indicated by initial capitalization. Grateful acknowledgment is given to the following for use of additional photographs: David Langley for the Steinway piano and the Volkswagen Beetle; The Checker Company for the Checker cab; The Harley Davidson Corporation; The Goodyear Corporation; International and The Cigarette Speed Boat Company.

Published by Crown Publishers, Inc., One Park Avenue, New York, New York 10016 and simultaneously in Canada by General Publishing Company Limited
Manufactured in the United States of America
Library of Congress Cataloging in Publication Data
Cornfeld, Betty.
    Quintessence: the quality of having it.

    1. Manufactures—Miscellanes. I. Edwards, Owen.
II. Title.
TS149.C67 1983   601'.3   83-7662
0-517-550903 (paper)
10 9 8 7 6 5 4 3 2
First Edition

For Oona B., Alex C., and Ezekiel E.
who are just what they ought to be

Sense and Quintessence

On a certain small island in Greece lives a certain man I know, in a style that can only be called exemplary. He is a rich man, v. rich as his English compatriots might say. But though there is nothing austere about the way he lives, neither is there anything ostentatious. He has painstakingly taught a local daughter the spells and conjurations of Provençal cooking, but he doesn't supplement the meager island food supply with air drops from Fortnum and Mason. He has installed an expensive electric pump to lift water from an ancient cistern to his lush garden, but he does all the planting himself and never sows a seed that's not native to the Mediterranean.   ☐ This man is a painter, and like most painters he is a materialist. Discerning the nature of things is second nature to him. He surrounds himself with things he has bought and found, from as far away as India and Tibet and as near as the tourist shop in the port village, some useful, some decorative, some so odd as to defy classification. Yet as different as they are, the painter's possessions always imply an elusive bond. Somehow, the capitol of a doric column found in a rubble wall near

Ephesus relates to a terra-cotta bowl of pebbles from a local beach, and a Breuer chair connects up with an empty Tuscan olive oil can used as a paint pot. Everything in sight is so unequivocally *right* in itself that it creates its own gravitational field, and in concert with all the other objects forms a soothingly harmonious system. To be around him and his possessions is to feel delightfully close to the center of something extraordinary and to be totally and inexplicably at home. ☐ This is a book about such things, things that offer more to us than we specifically ask of them and to which we respond more strongly than is easily explained. What the various things in this book have in common—whether candy or cars, cigarettes or shoes, baseball bats or blimps—is the quality of *quintessence*. In a wide variety of ways, they each exhibit a rare and mysterious capacity to be just exactly what they ought to be. ☐ The pleasure such things offer us is wonderful and illogical; it is very like the pure joy a child feels when he unexpectedly comes into the possession of something magically desirable. The power of quintessential things—however simple or sophisticated, however carefully designed or accidentally apt—is imponderable but undeniable. ☐ Although quintessence cannot be found in abundance in our claptrap age, its ancient voice still whispers beneath modern exteriors and we do well to recognize it and seek it out. For while we may use quintessential things for commonplace purposes, they serve as talismans and guideposts, touching our souls with souls of their own. ☐ That inanimate objects might have souls may make us uncomfortable, conjuring up such bad business as virgins sacrificed to glowering statues or pernicious spirits lurking in trees and stones, but there's no avoiding the idea. Throughout the ages a kind of magic has inhabited things—stones and staffs, mirrors and rings and chalices—that rationalists have railed against in vain and, not infrequently, at their peril. When, for instance, Byzantine Emperor Leo III ordered the destruction of all religious icons in his realm to stamp out the then rampant practice of having painted saints serve as godparents at baptisms, he set off a rebellion that cost him, along with the lives of many dutiful bureaucrats, the invaluable loyalty of the materialistic vassal state of Venice. ☐ The numinous nature of inanimate things has always caused anguish for someone. Pascal, for one, lamented that his friends, "upon seeing some pleasant object, have given themselves up and attached themselves to it." Poor Pascal, so downhearted at the humanity in others and in himself. His is the ancient cry of the desert anchorite, seeing devils in every golden bowl and the apocalypse in every bolt of silk. Yet it's a safe bet that lying near Pascal's hand as he wrote these words was some favorite thing—a skull, an ivory sphere, a silver-handled fly whisk, a carved marble inkwell—without which life might have seemed less well formed. But what Pascal might not have wanted to admit, a more lenient Frenchman, Marcel Proust, put nicely in a description of M. Swann's not-at-all-miserable situation: "He felt, when his mind dwelt upon his brilliant connections, the same external support, the same solid comfort as when he looked at the fine estate, the fine silver, the fine table linen which had come down to him from his forebears." Even in his cork-lined room Proust wasn't put off by Swann for his sense of comfort derived from the things around him; he understood it perfectly. ☐ If our possessions have the capacity to define us, as many philosophers have claimed, it stands to reason that those same things should be, in themselves, well defined. They should have the quality of quintessence, showing clearly what Kant called "the thing in the thing." ☐ The modern definition of quintessence is "the pure, highly concentrated essence of something." But a truer meaning was given to the word by medieval philosophers: "The fifth and highest essence (after the four elements of earth, air, fire, and water), thought to be the substance of the heavenly bodies and latent in all things." In other words, something quite like a soul. By this definition we can presume that the more of that precious fifth essence a given object—or person or place—has, the higher its standing on the ladder of virtue. ☐ In the Middle Ages, of course, the idea that quintessence was latent in everything might have seemed self-evident; all things were either made by the hand of God (from mountains to swallows' nests) or by the hand of man. Quintessence might manifest itself surprisingly in the wooden mortar of a peasant, for instance, rather than in the blown-glass vessel of a master craftsman—but it was always a possibility and easy to believe in. With the advent of mass production, the odds against quintessence grew and have continued to grow. The craftsman's skill played a smaller and smaller part in the manufacture of the ordinary things that people bought and used, and uniformity and efficiency replaced the slow and often enchanted variations of handwork. Since the Industrial Revolution it has become possible to assume that quintessence is inconsistent with mass production, and the premise is hard to deny. The difference between, say, a hand-knitted sweater and one knitted by machine is easy to see, and it's no feat to find a thousand other examples of that difference. But the decreased probability of something's being quintessential doesn't mean the possibility no longer exists. Quintessence lives, as vitally as ever; it's just harder to discern amid the un-distinguished plenty of our times. ☐ One of the great dilemmas of our age is that while the powerful magic of advertising makes us want more, what we end up with, we love less. Constantly promised satisfaction, unable to find it, we become drifters from one failed possession to the next, not so much materialists (that much misunderstood and unfairly maligned term) as "thingists." Disenchantment comes with this territory, and

an unhappy kind of lust to possess more and more, as if the emptiness of things without soul can be made up for by sheer excess. Instead, our sense of loss is merely multiplied.   ☐ In *The Context of No Context* George Trow points out that "the idea of choice is easily debased if one forgets that the aim is *to have chosen successfully,* not to be endlessly choosing." To choose successfully, one must be able to seek out things that are not only perfectly appropriate for their functions, but also exhibit, in John Ruskin's phrase, the "mysterious sense of unaccountable life in things themselves."   ☐ Because they are animated by these dual virtues of functional aptitude and inner vivacity, quintessential things don't lose their power to fulfill us as we grow accustomed to them. They are as right as they can be. As a result, they provide a way off the many and various wheels of thingism. One might, for instance, become obsessed with having the right watch—watches being potently symbolic as well as practical—and end up with half a dozen, loving each for a period of weeks, or months, until one begins to look for something just a little bit more perfect. But if we know enough to search out a *quintessential* watch, something will happen that goes beyond simply the having of a watch. This is what was nicely described by John Cheever when he wrote in *Oh, What a Paradise It Seems,* "The fleetness he felt on skates seemed to have the depth of an ancient experience." Quintessential things give off that sort of echo. They tap into an ancient source of strength—an abiding rightness—that makes them unimprovable. A quintessential watch can get you off the wheel of watches—you will have chosen well, so you no longer need to go on choosing. There are many wheels to thingism, and there are quintessential things to get us off most of them.   ☐ How do you know quintessence? The best answer is the simplest and the most difficult: You know it because you know it. To the receptive soul, quintessence reveals itself. Our instincts react to quintessence whether or not our intellects understand it. In your heart, you know it's right, and in your brain, without understanding why, a voice declares "That's it!" The trick to being receptive is to train your instinct by trusting it; the more attuned to quintessence you become, the more easily you recognize it. And despite the constant static given off by all the wrong stuff a desperate economy thrusts at us, quintessence is always there to be found. It is the good news, shining through the bad.   ☐ People and places are quintessential, as well as things. They are rare, given the ceaseless outpouring of trash architecture and here-and-gone celebrities that characterize the late twentieth century, but they survive. Look around. Fred Astaire is quintessential. So is Mickey Mouse. The Pyramids, the Parthenon, and the Chrysler Building are quintessential. As are Johnny Carson, the Concord jet, the '38 Cord (if you can find one), and Charo (if you can find *her*). Wrigley Field is quintessential and so is the Rose Bowl. Cary Grant is eminently quintessential, along with Mick Jagger and that other symbol of pure sex, the White Rock girl. Helen Gurley Brown and her immaculate conception, that Cosmo Girl, are sisters in quintessence. Jack Dempsey was quintessential and Ali is quintessential still. Sienna and Vienna are quintessential, as are Paris and Peking and the music of Mozart. ☐ In the days of the star system in Hollywood, the quality of quintessence was what made true stars and raised them above celebrities or simply well-known actors. Mae West was quintessential. And Laurel and Hardy. And Gary Cooper, Humphrey Bogart, George Sanders, Ingrid Bergman, Charlie McCarthy, Peter Lorre, and, of course, Marilyn Monroe. ☐ At certain times politicians are quintessential, and whether we like it or not, those tend to be interesting times. Churchill was quintessential, and Roosevelt, and De Gaulle, and Tito, and George Patton, probably for the better, as were, very much for the worse, Hitler and Stalin. ☐ In more recent times, the public pickings are decidedly slimmer. Everett Dirksen was quintessential, so too George Wallace, Jimmy Hoffa, William Buckley, and Billy Graham. But the political star system seems to have gone the way of the Hollywood version. Perhaps the world has grown too frightening for us to want larger-than-life pols, but as the guns get bigger our big guns seem strangely diminished. ☐ Quintessential people rise above the crowd by virtue of their charismatic personalities, and quintessential places blend harmoniously with the landscapes of our souls, but how can we unerringly distinguish quintessential things? Besides the instinctual tendency to recognize such things because they simply are what they are, there *are* signposts that point to quintessence. Thomas Hardy described great mathematics as having "a very high degree of unexpectedness, combined with inevitability and economy." The same may be said of quintessential things. Even though they may at some point have seemed unusual, even revolutionary, the way they are now appears self-evident, and you can't imagine how such a thing—the Volkswagen Beetle, let's say—could be other than it is. More important, you don't *want* to imagine it any other way, so the idea of improvement becomes irrelevant. Rarely does a quintessential thing survive improvement. It may get better in terms of function—as has the trimmer, less-arrogant car, the modern Rolls-Royces—but almost invariably in gaining a competitive edge, it loses its magical rightness. ☐ A quintessential thing cannot be made more quintessential; it either is or it isn't, and if it is, tampering won't do a bit of good and may ruin everything. The Oreo cookie is just exactly what it ought to be, quintessential, unimprovable. But a few years ago someone at Nabisco—some bright enterpriser who just didn't get it—decided that to build a better Oreo all you had to do was double the amount of sweet stuff in the middle. That's what kids love, isn't it? The result

was a catastrophe, as dead wrong as the original Oreo was dead right. Nabisco, a company that makes few mistakes, has yet to admit this blunder and goes on marketing their woeful "Double Stuff." No doubt somebody eats them, but devotees of the quintessential Oreo are not amused.   ☐ However clever a design or vaunted a purpose, quintessence can no more be stalked and captured than can true love. Either it occurs, or it doesn't; and often it comes when least expected, or fails to appear when most desperately desired. But when it does appear, quintessence changes everything. The Frisbee might have come and gone on the merciless tide of trendiness like the hula hoop. Both were round, plastic, essentially useless. And of the two, the hula hoop attracted far more notoriety. But after thirty years, the quintessential Frisbee is still very much with us, while the hapless hoop shows up only in documentaries on "Those Fabulous Fifties."   ☐ The "inevitability" of a quintessential object may be recognized in the feeling it gives that the thing itself wants to look the way it does. The Italian auto designer Sergio Pininfarina, creator of the Ferrari Dino (and son of the man who designed the legendary Cisitalia, the only car displayed at The Museum of Modern Art) has said that a good designer "designs steel as steel likes to be designed"; and in just that way, a quintessential thing tends to look as if it conceived itself. In other words, if a lighter wants to look like a lighter, it will look like a Zippo; if a building wants to look like a skyscraper, it will look like the Empire State Building, and so on.   ☐ Pininfarina calls great design a victory for "the personal pencil," and more often than not there is in quintessence the pared-down line of a pencil sketch. A rule of thumb often useful in determining whether something is quintessential or not is whether it resembles a child's drawing of the thing. Ask a three-year-old to draw a dog and the kid will draw a bullterrier. A child's drawing of a car will look like a Checker. And, one presumes, a child's sketch of a bottle of champagne would be very like Dom Perignon.   ☐ Ultimately, the way to recognize quintessence is by the spiritual kinship it engenders; a quintessential thing reaches you instantly on an uncluttered emotional level, and, like a good and oft-told tale, it satisfies in ways both new and older than memory.   ☐ These are difficult times for true materialists. The outpouring of trash and trifles and soulless status symbols complicates the search for satisfaction in abiding objects. The sirens of thingism call to us incessantly, seductive and ultimately destructive. But rather than stopping our ears, we have to open our eyes to the quintessence in the people and places—and especially the things—capable of getting us off wheel after wheel, and wheels after that.   ☐ The objects in this book are not meant to serve as a buyer's catalogue, but rather as a guide to the recognition of quintessence as it manifests itself in the products of modern methodology. With few exceptions, they are mass-produced, and almost all are currently available in the marketplace. Some may not be specifically useful to a given reader, but their utility is not solely the point here. Without a child or two around, the Slinky toy might not seem a necessary part of life, but whether you play with it or not, the thing itself is as beautiful as any sculpture. Milk-Bone dog biscuits may seem something for dog owners only, but they'll hold their own on any shelf of pre-Columbian art. Can anyone but Goodyear afford to keep a blimp patched and flying? Perhaps not, but how sad to forgo the pleasure of taking full possession of it for those slow, wonderful moments when it's floating overhead. There are many more quintessential things than appear here. No attempt has been made to provide the definitive collection that incorporates all quintessence, nor could that be done. These things are simply indications of how quintessence can manifest itself and how to know it when you see it. Categories aren't meant to be inferred either. The VW Beetle isn't *the* quintessential car; it's just quintessential. For everyone who may agree that Fox's U-Bet is the quintessential chocolate syrup, there will be someone else who leaps to his feet and shouts "Bosco," or "Hershey's," and we are having no part of that melee.   ☐ What this book is *not* is a list of what's best. Worrying about what is the best of anything is thingism at its most delusory, since, inevitably, the best of today is bettered tomorrow. A life defined by having the best is a life of endless choosing and endless letdowns. This book came to be when two old friends met by accident at Scribner's bookstore on Fifth Avenue in New York and admitted to each other that though it probably wasn't the best bookstore around, Scribner's is just exactly what a bookstore ought to be. Possibly nothing in this book is the best of its category. "Best" is a judgment based on statistics, not taste or instinct; and in a world of constant technological innovation and furious competition, being the best of anything is usually a short-term occupation. Quintessential things are blissfully beyond all that. They are faithful and durable and *hors de combat*. The reason they matter so much is that they don't have to wave a tacky foam-rubber finger in the air and honk "We're No. 1!" Quintessence is sublime, a piece of the True Rock and it's here today and here tomorrow—o.e.

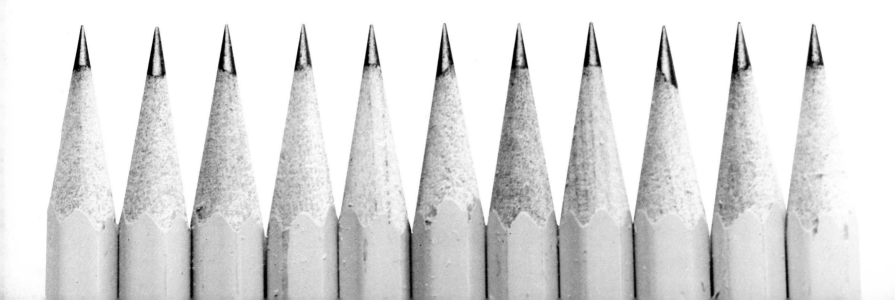

QUINTESSENCE

The Martini

Crystal clear, chill, restorative, the queen of cocktails is as virtuous as a virgin spring. It is also a symbol of worldly wisdom and power; not for nothing is it the preferred drink of James Bond (though his insistence that it be shaken, not stirred, *is* capricious). Through all the calls for tequila sunrises and banana daiquiris

and kirs, the firmly spoken order, "Martini, straight up, not *too* dry" cuts like an enchanted sword.

Unlike many classics, the martini is not *sui generis* but has evolved slowly to its present high level of civilization. The drink first appeared in 1862 in Professor Jerry Thomas's *Bon Vivant's Companion* as the Martinez, essentially a tumbler of vermouth with a pony of gin tossed in along with bitters, maraschino liqueur, a slice of lemon, and ice. By the end of the century the name had become the martini, and vermouth and gin were in equal parts. The drink dried up over the years until reaching the classic (and still delectable) formulation of four parts gin to one of vermouth, with a twist of lemon or an olive. Though overbreeding has led to such limp nonsense as merely spraying the glass with vermouth, more pungent levels of the wine are making a comeback.

As a surcease from the stresses of a petty world, there is nothing quite like it. Here's looking at *you*, Señor Martinez, whoever you were.

The Ace Comb

Remember Buzz? Sure you do. Buzz was the infinitely cool leader of the pack in *Rebel Without a Cause* who gave James Dean such a hard time until ill-advisedly driving himself off a cliff in a memorable game of wheel-to-wheel chicken. To any clean-cut teenage boy of the fifties, Buzz was awesome and enviable at

smooth back the left side, with the left hand following along to catch any errant wisps. And then on to the right side with the left hand over to complete the job.

The *de rigueur* comb for this little macho moment was—and is—the Ace, with its just right name and perfectly handy size and its wide- and fine-tooth ends. (The wide-tooth end, on properly mulched hair, can leave glistening corrugated rows

that keep their shape for hours, or even days.) The Ace has come a long way; it has been tucked into countless bathing suit waistbands since its first hard-rubber incarnation came out of the American Company in Booneville, Arkansas, in the dark ages B.E. (Before Elvis). The comb has traveled from one corporation to another over the years—Nabisco even owned Ace for a few years, probably until someone tried to eat one. During its travels, the comb changed from hard rubber to plastic and seems to have lost most of its history. But while many of its generation have shed their hair, Ace hasn't lost a tooth—it's still the best in the business. Just add Wildroot, Kreml, Brylcreem, or the hair dressing of your choice, and let the comb do its stuff.

the same time. Even though he lost out on the chicken run, he was just the guy all the other guys wanted to be in their slightly greasy heart of hearts.　□ And do you remember what Buzz did before his last ride? He combed his hair with that quintessential gesture of the fifties—comb in right hand, hand over head to

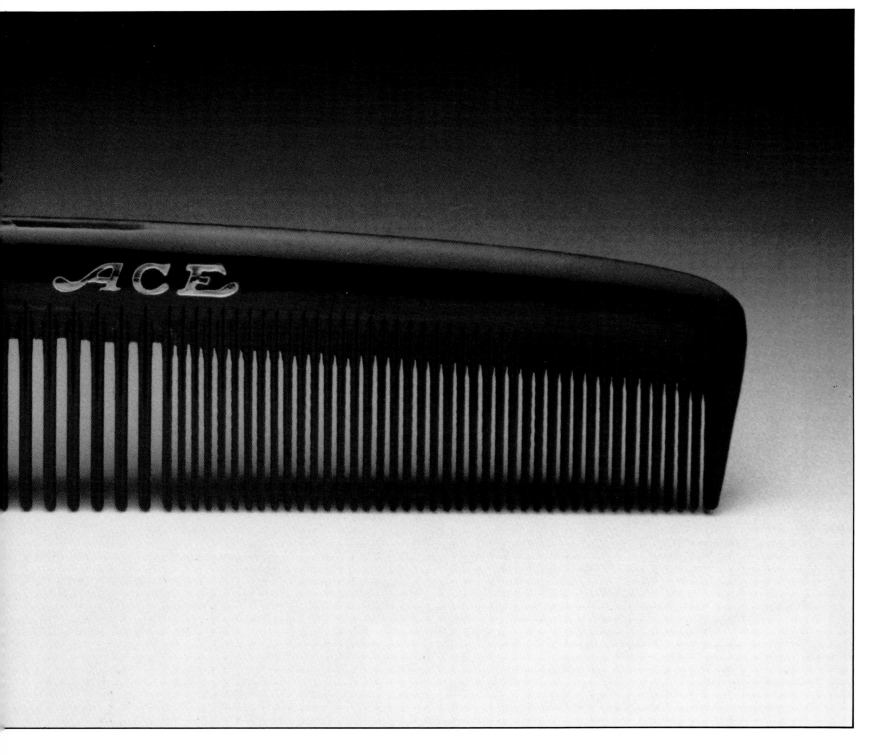

Wedgwood Plain White Bone China

The latest trend in French cuisine is to lighter food in smaller portions, served with a spare beauty that teeters between elegance and austerity. So what else is *nouvelle?* Hard-pressed English nobility have been eating that way for years, with one lamb chop and a nouveau potato or two served on the

serene white perfection of Wedgwood. This white bone china lends new richness to the word plain. It is so aesthetically unconfused that even if you leave the table with your stomach unfilled, your soul will have supped well.

Bone china was first produced by the Wedgwood factory during the era of Josiah Wedgwood II, son of the founder, between the years of 1812 and 1822. As the term implies the whiteness and lightweight strength of the plates come from the inclusion of pulverized animal bone in the clay, augmented by china stone. To be called bone china, at least half of the mix must be bone. Although Wedgwood security about their formula is a lot tighter than that of Buckingham Palace of late, the company will reveal that the amount of ox bone in their china is well over 50 percent, which gives it a polar whiteness and unusual strength. In fact, Wedgwood claims that four of their after-dinner coffee cups, one under each tire, can support the weight of a car—though what sort of car, or why you might want to do such a thing, is not made clear.

The Spalding Rubber Ball

A ball, in order properly to be a ball, must be round and must bounce. Nothing seems quite so round and bouncy as a Spalding pink rubber ball. Its size is perfect for hands large or small; its appearance at rest or at play charms the eye with pure functional simplicity. Made of unadorned hard rubber, the ball

is firm, which gives it sincerity, the promise of a true and noble bounce. And, of no small importance, it makes a satisfying *thwok* on sidewalk or stoop. There's no knowing how many great baseball careers have started with the wonderful rightness of this little pink ball.

The Spalding Company manufactures other things besides the pink rubber ball, and everything else the company makes is said to be a Spalding this or a Spalding that. But the pink rubber ball—and only the pink rubber ball—is a Spald*een* (spelled Spalding in elegant script on the ball itself). And anyone who doesn't know *that* can't really know why the Spaldeen is The Ball.

Ivory Soap

The invention of 99 and $^{44}/_{100}$ percent pure Ivory soap was 100 percent pure accident. A worker at the Proctor and Gamble plant left the mixing machinery on during his lunch break, which whipped a lot of air into the soap ingredients. Unknowingly, Proctor and his cousin, Gamble, shipped out a batch of

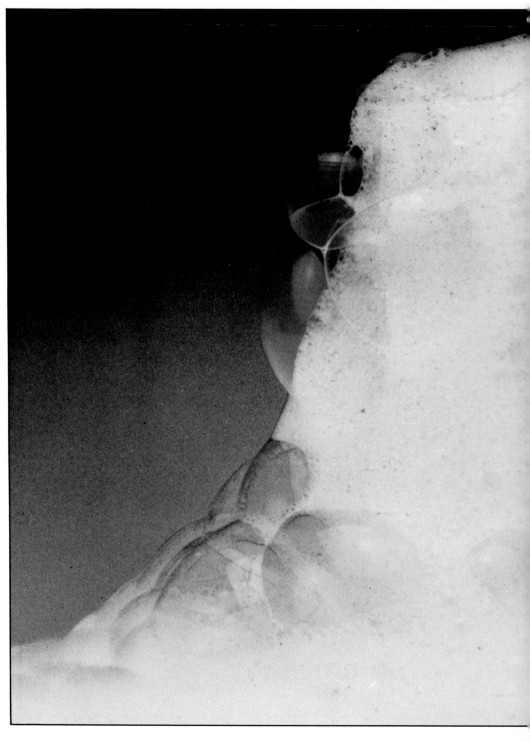

confluence of conscious and subconscious, he hears the preacher read the Forty-fifth Psalm: "All thy garments smell of myrrh and aloes and cassia out of ivory palaces whereby they have made thee glad." Whereby they have made Harley glad.

In December 1882, after naming his soap, Harley Proctor sent samples to a number of chemists, asking them to compare it to the competition. One of those chemists found that Ivory had only $^{56}/_{100}$ths of a percent of impurities (even less than castile, the most popular soap of the day), and one of the great ad slogans of all time was born. Ivory is still just what Proctor wanted it to be—dependable, indispensable, and economical. Its wrapper is cheerful, innocent, and, above all, clean—the white bar floats between blue waves, with a single red wave to catch your eye like a flag. Even the waxiness of the paper echoes what's waiting securely within. The shiny white bar lathers into an instant slithery richness. Wash with a bar of Ivory and there's no question that something is going on here. This soap is working. After you've washed your hands and dried them, your hands smell clean—not disinfected or perfumed—just clean. All this *and* . . . it floats. And swims and bobs and comes back up from the depths. A bath toy that no one can make fun of.

floating soap. And, if it's to be believed, the story behind the naming of the soap is 100 percent pure, period. The year is 1879, Harley Proctor is sitting in church, half listening to the sermon, half pondering what to name his company's new White Soap (its highly unoriginal original name). Then, in a perfect

Campbell's Tomato Soup

Canned soup is a must for every cupboard and every bomb shelter. The idea of canning condensed soups originated in 1897 with Arthur Dorrance, nephew of Dr. J. T. Dorrance, partner of Joseph Campbell, founder of the firm that bears his name. (When Campbell retired in 1900, he took himself and left his name.)

Tomato soup was the very first condensed soup the company manufactured, and it remains the best of its many offerings. The soup, when reconstituted with milk, tastes as thick, rich, and creamy as homemade. The instructions do state that you can make it with water, but that's like saying you can make "s'mores" with Ritz crackers. Adding a can of milk transforms this thick red glop into a pale, salmon-colored potful of soup that is at once soothing and delicious. Once you've started eating, you'll never wish you'd had a sandwich instead. Tomato soup always delivers.

And we don't need Andy Warhol to tell us that the can is a work of art. In terms of iconography, the red and white colors on the label are borrowed from the colors of Cornell's football uniforms; and the gold medallion was added in 1900, the year that Campbell's Soups won the Gold Medal for Excellence at the Paris Exposition. Campbell's makes many other soup varieties besides tomato, But basic is best. Whether you say tomahto or we say tomayto, it's mmmmm ... great.

The Peanut Butter and Jelly Sandwich

What the crêpe is to France, moussaka to Greece, and goulash to Hungary, the peanut butter and jelly sandwich is to America. Never mind that no one has ever figured out which wine is just right with a pb&j or that it's not in the *Joy of Cooking*; it is the staple of staples, manna from mamma, this country's version

of the playing fields of Eton. McDonald's may brag of 40 billion served, but the number of pb&js that have vanished into American children at lunch is surely beyond calculation.

It might not seem that something as elemental as the peanut butter and jelly sandwich would have a recipe, but it does. In fact, the ingredients *must not* be varied if the concoction is to succeed on all levels (it is not, after all, just something to eat). *The* pb&j is made with (and only with) Skippy smooth peanut butter, Welch's grape jelly, and a well-known white bread whose only other legitimate use is as emergency play dough. The sad, flabby stuff bears only the faintest resemblance to bread as most of the world knows it, and yet it serves the key ingredients with the slavish devotion of a mute eunuch in the Byzantine court. Have you ever tried peanut butter and jelly on rye? And as for chunky peanut butter, or strawberry preserves . . . why put on airs?

The Timex Mercury 20521 Watch

A watch is a device used for telling time. It is there, on your wrist, to tell you at a glance to walk slower or faster. The plain white-faced, water-resistant Timex Mercury with the easy-to-read black Arabic numerals and sweep second hand is pure function. It tells you the time, and that's all it does. The face even

has minute lines between the big numbers, so that you can know that it's thirteen minutes and thirty-two seconds after four.

Digital watches tell you that, too. But they won't tell anybody else. (Have you ever tried to sneak a glance at someone's digital watch?) And time moves too swiftly and inexorably on a digital watch. The numbers rush on, and in the time you've watched them change, part of you is dying. Metaphysically speaking, digitals are just too oppressive. As for quartz watches, they don't get wound and they don't tick. And without the tick they might as well be recording time on another planet.

The Timex Company was originally U.S. Time, a producer of time fuses and torpedo gyroscopes for antiaircraft and precision instruments. U.S. Time's president, Joakim Lehmkuhl, thought up the idea of creating an inexpensive and sturdy watch and brought what was then an heirloom commodity into the twentieth-century world of expendability. (Did you ever know anyone who's had a Timex repaired? It goes until it doesn't, and then you just up and buy a new one. Of course, a Timex Mercury can be repaired, but at $16.95 why bother?) When Timex watches first came on the market in 1949, the public was appropriately leery of the concept of a cheap watch. A watch that cost less than $20 could never be expected to run for even as long as it took you to get home. So Timex advised its salesmen to demonstrate the watch's durability by throwing it against walls and on floors. And if all that wasn't proof enough, Timex hired newsman John Cameron Swayze to torture the watch. Like some South American dictator, Swayze subjected the watch to any number of hair-raising tests, but it took the licking and kept on ticking. Timex marches on.

The Steinway Piano

If there's one thing you don't associate with a Steinway, it's the kitchen. But to those in the piano-know, the two are indeed related. For the so-called kitchen piano is the forerunner of the modern piano. And it is so named because Henry Englehard Steinwig built it in his kitchen in Seesen, Germany. By the time

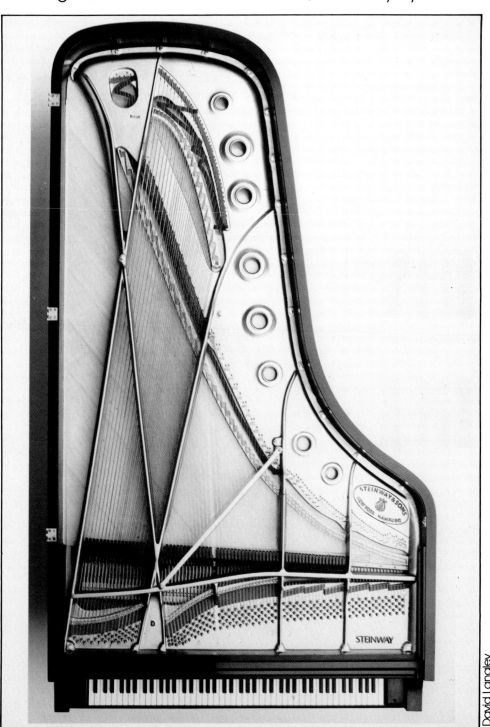

he came to America and founded a piano company with his sons in 1853, Steinwig had become Steinway. A Steinway (to say Steinway piano is almost a redundancy) is known as "The Instrument of the Immortals." And so it is. It is the piano of choice for (among many others) Rudolf Serkin, Andre Watts, Misha Dichter, Vladimir Ashkenazy, Lili Kraus, Vladimir Horowitz. And *was* the piano of choice for the late Artur Rubinstein.

No matter where in America a pianist has a concert, he can find a Steinway within a finger's reach. The company maintains 305 of them (about $7 million worth) expressly for performance use. The artist must pay to have the piano tuned up and moved to the hall, but the use of the Steinway is free. (It's been reported that if a pianist should ever elect to play a recital on anything other than a Steinway, Steinway will forever refuse to deliver one of its concert pianos to him.) Only immortals may play these instruments on concert stages, but even mere mortals can own them. But with a price tag as high as $28,000 (that's for their very best, the Model D Concert Grand) and a wait of maybe as much as a year, it's hardly an impulse purchase. A Steinway is a serious investment, and well it should be. It's one of the most carefully crafted instruments in the world. These ivories are not for tickling. No ticklers need apply.

Camel Cigarettes

Being a smoker used to mean never having to say you were sorry. Smoking was not only *done* but it was done with real style. Nobody ever pretended it was good for you, but to smoke with grace and elegance was a sign of a virtue that counted for more than mere clean living. In fact, smoking a real cigarette gave

come a long way, baby, toward joining the inestimably grown-up.

In those days of forthright smoking, cigarettes didn't apologize, either. They didn't hide their elemental natures under names like Merit, True, Vantage, even (for God's sake) Satin. There were giants in the ashtray then, Pall Malls, Chesterfields, Lucky Strikes (stunning in green and gold). Best of all there were—and still are—Camels, the

powerful, pungent, basic smokes that are America's answer to such classic weeds as Balkan Sobranies and Galoises. Since they were first introduced by R.J. Reynolds in 1913, Camels have been the true smoker's cigarette. Untainted by menthol, undistorted by needless extra centimeters, Camels have entered the age of interchangeable cigarettes and boutique smoking with their integrity intact. And so has the Camel pack, a wonderful pocket-sized evocation of the exotic Middle East whose design closely resembles—except for the placement of the palm trees and the pyramid—an 1820 etching by a French artist named de Sèvres. At its best, smoking ought to imply worldliness and at least the possibility of romance; the Camel pack does the job without so much as an inhale. And the unfiltered cigarette lets you do the things a smoker ought to—from tamping down the loose shreds of tobacco (deftly, six times, on a thumbnail) to discreetly picking that one errant bit off the tip of the tongue. Camel, we light up your leaf.

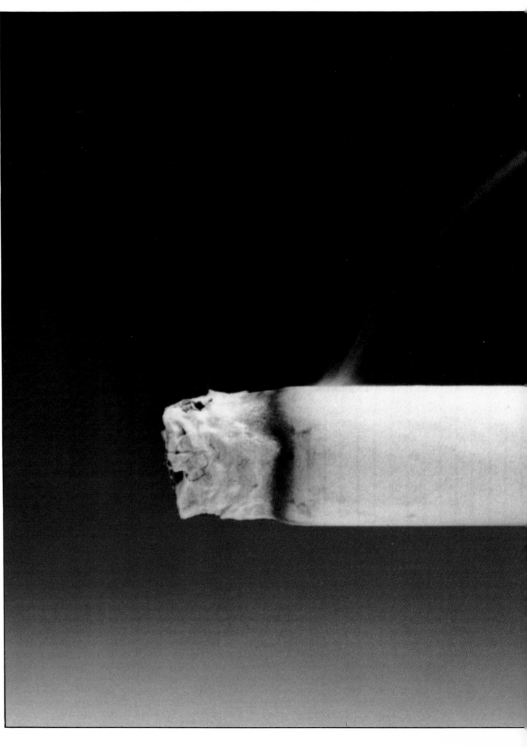

any man, woman, and the occasional red-faced, gasping adolescent several chances daily to exhibit, quite literally, grace under fire. If you could fill your lungs with the sort of substance that could kill a 200-pound fireman and at the same time tap off an ash with a gesture befitting a Balinese dancer, you had

Keds High-top Sneakers

By the narrowest sort of definition Keds black high tops are shoes, a practical matter of inexpensive protection for the feet. But they are far, far more: a foundation, a bedrock, a fundament as uncompromised and dependable as a first principle of physics. Noble and comfortable, Keds have a look of inevitability, as if

they just had to happen and therefore did. ("Let there be sneakers!")

It might seem that once Charles Goodyear managed to vulcanize rubber in the 1860s shoes of rubber would logically follow, yet he might as easily have vulcanized hats. But as good luck and the inescapable logic of fate would have it, the end of the nineteenth century brought the first rubber and canvas shoe. Keds came on the scene somewhat later, around 1917, and arrived not in their formal black, but in prosaic brown.

Keds were the first sneaker to be popularly marketed, and the name represents a prototypical marketing ploy. The root for the name is *ped*, Latin for foot. But in its wisdom U.S. Rubber had decided that the letter *K* had some unexplainable, magical appeal. The change was made, and the age of Kedophilia was upon us, giving birth to the shoes your big brother told you you'd never be big enough to fill. The high-tech allure of running shoes has cast a temporary shadow on these temples for the feet, but nothing can replace them. Here's looking at you, Ked!

The Oreo Cookie

Oh, Oh, Oreo.
Nabisco claims it's the world's most popular cookie, and why not? The Oreo has been around since 1913, when it made its debut as the Oreo Biscuit. In 1921 it was renamed the Oreo Sandwich and

renamed yet again in 1948 when it became the Oreo Creme Sandwich, its current designation.

The Oreo is more than a cookie (as profound a thing as a cookie is); it is a form of personal expression. You can eat it straightforwardly as a sandwich inviolate; or you can lift the top off, eat that, then scrape the sweet white stuff off the second wafer with your front teeth, then give the bottom wafer to someone you're not that crazy about. Or you can eat the top wafer and then the cream and second wafer together. Or you can eat the cream first and throw the cookie away. Or you can . . .

The quintessentiality of the Oreo is mysteriously and precariously balanced; witness the failure of the spin-off Oreo Double Stuff, the Jaws II of cookies, in which the white cream is laid on twice as thickly as it ought to be: a classic case of fixing something that isn't broken. The real Oreo, having twice the biscuit as icing, brilliantly fulfills a fundamental requirement for the quintessential cookie: It absolutely demands to be eaten with milk.

The Mont Blanc Diplomat Pen

If you have only one life to sign away, for self-pity's sake do the deed with a tool worthy of the moment, the Mont Blanc Meisterstuck No. 149—a.k.a. the Diplomat (though Grand Inquisitor might fit just as well). If the pen is indeed mightier than the sword, that pen is surely the Diplomat. Everything about it is

difference between preparing to write by pressing a ballpoint's button and slowly unscrewing the top of a Diplomat, removing it and replacing it at the other end, then pausing just another moment in an attitude the manufacturer nicely calls "classical pensiveness." If by then your banker is not ready to extend far more credit than you're worth, the man is dead to

style. (The effect on subordinates of this stern swagger stick of pens is daunting in the extreme. The tiny "Germany" engraved on the pen's uppermost gold ring comes as no surprise.)

The Mont Blanc Company began manufacturing fountain pens very much like the Diplomat in 1908, when the company's president, a certain Herr Dzianbor, grew tired of traveling around Germany with a bottle of ink to dip his pen in. In those days the written word was king, the typewriter was a slightly contemptible convenience, and the time was not envisioned when the act of writing would be brutally parodied by "word processors" capable of neither blot nor blessing. With the Diplomat poised, even today, there is still no need to think about such things.

significant, from its howitzer shell heft to its profound blackness, from the six-pointed trademark snow-cap (left off pens sold in Arab countries because of its resemblance to the Star of David) to the 14-karat gold nib engraved with the number 4810—the height in meters of Mont Blanc.   □ Consider the

Frederick's of Hollywood Lingerie

Open this catalogue and you return to a world that never was. Its illustrated glamour girls, with their Dolly Parton figures and Barbie Doll hairdos, are reminiscent of comic-book heroines of the fifties. Frederick's has been around since 1946, and the "sin-sational" illusions he created then haven't

changed through all the ideological upheavals in the meantime. Everything that Frederick Mellinger creates is the purest form of what he represents. It's naughty, gaudy, and superannuated. King Frederick rules a country whose citizenry has never heard of feminism, and if they did, could only ask, "But why?" Frederick's garments, according to their maker, are "designed the way a *man* wants to see a woman and the way a *woman* wants to see her reflection in the mirror." Half of Frederick's premise, we're sure, is true, and on this truth he has created a business that brings well over $20 million a year. While there are 117 Frederick's stores in thirty states, the biggest one, and certainly the best, is the

headquarters on Hollywood Boulevard, the architectural equivalent of a Busby Berkley production number. But Frederick's is mainly a mail (male?) order business. The catalogue beckons you: "Catch Him by Surprise"; "Make a Breakthrough to Love, Sex Appeal, and a Stunning New You"; "Burst onto the Scene 'n Be the Girl of His Dreams." Innocent prurience. The pages are thick with fantasy. Concept by Hefner, adaptation by Disney. See "The Living End" . . . "Its miracle lift shelf raises fanny UP and OUT." Or "The Cadillac" . . . "It takes a small bust and pushes it UP with 2-way in-up, push-up action for deep, alluring CLEAVAGE."

There are teddys of every description. Corsets. Bare-nipple bras. Garter belts. Crotchless panties. They're made of Spandex, lurex, tricot, lamé (both silver and gold), and marabou feathers. Lots of marabou. Frederick's alone could render the marabou an endangered species. But, then again, he's certainly doing everything he can to preserve that most endangered species of all—the sex kitten.

The Slinky Toy

Technically speaking, it's a spring with zero compression and zero tension. It demonstrates two principles of physics: Hooke's law, which states that a body tends to return to its original shape after it's been stretched, and the law of inertia, the tendency of a body in motion to stay in motion in a straight line

unless disturbed by an external force. Richard James, the man who sprung Slinky, was a marine engineer well schooled in these principles. While experimenting with coiled springs in an attempt to discover a way to protect a ship's delicate instruments from vibration, lo and behold, one of the springs fell from a shelf above his desk. As James watched, the spring landed on a row of books and proceeded to drop, coil following coil, from one book to another, until it finally fell to the floor. Bathwater, apples, coiled springs—if you're in the right place at the right time with the right mind, you can discover some pretty amazing things.

In fact, this little discovery of an animate spring became the Rubik's Cube of the late forties. But unlike Rubik's Cube, the hula hoop, or the Frisbee, one need have no mental agility or physical ability to enjoy the Slinky. Hold one end of this splendid creation in each of your hands and, pushing up one end and then the other, feel the gentle pull of its arc and become attuned to the soaring rhythm of its movements. It's like juggling without risk. Or lift one hand

ever so slowly above the other and watch the Slinky ripple deliberately toward its other half until it suddenly flops onto itself, whole again. This pleasurable experience is one to be had only with the metal Slinky. The many-colored plastic Slinky, while it offers safe enjoyment for a child, has neither the weight nor the smooth movement of the genuine article.

The Slinky was named by the discoverer's wife, Betty. She called it a Slinky because she thought it both stealthy and furtive. The truth is, the thing descends the stairs in such a stately, plump manner that it might better have been called the Buck Mulligan. To watch it make its own way from one floor to the next offers the same fascination as watching a raindrop travel hesitantly down a windowpane. But the Slinky never threatens disappointment. The aforementioned law of inertia guarantees that it will get to the bottom of the landing, and maybe even a bit beyond. No grown-up goes out to buy himself a Slinky, but just come upon one by accident, or get one for a gift, and you're in *its* hands before it's in yours.

The Brown Paper Bag

Forget the International Style. Compared to the austere clarity of the great American brown bag, the architecture of the Seagram Building is hopelessly rococo. The luxurious beauty of the basic material itself eloquently restates the miracle of paper and is no less pleasing than the finest Rives Arches. Picasso

painted on the stuff; Saul Steinberg has used it to create memorable masks. And we all receive its grace every time we take a sandwich off to work. The bag is such a fundamental part of the American way that it has contributed the verb "to brown-bag" to our language.

The bag pictured here is the Union Camp Tiger #6, chosen partly for the fineness of its paper, partly for the pluckiness of its name, but mostly because one of the authors of this book spent a couple of years across the savannahs from a plant where bags such as this were made and grew perversely fond of their distinctive natal aroma.

One of the most delightful things about the brown bag, other than its architecture, is its capacity to look just as good used as new. Like snowflakes, no two bags crease just the same way, and with each use the paper takes on a silkier softness and a more fascinating patina of dark stains. Throwing out a brown paper bag after only one use is not only wasteful, it's artistically reprehensible.

The Milk-Bone Dog Biscuit

Anything is capable of becoming a fad, even a pet. (Pets are so faddish that some entrepreneurial genius successfully marketed pet rocks.) The Lhasa apso was the decorator dog for a while. Then the Kheeshond. Then the Akita. And even if your dog isn't "in," his life-style can be. He can be lodged at one of the new dog

hotels. Or he can go to a dog analyst. Designer dog foods will no doubt soon be upon us (Adolfopo, Klein-L-Ration, Karl Lagerfeld for Collie), but these too shall pass. No matter what "in" dog item comes along, Milk-Bone will still be around.

First made in 1908 by the F.H. Bennett Biscuit Company, a small bakery on New York's Lower East Side, the Milk-Bone is what bones are supposed to look like, but almost never do. Originally made from cereals, minerals, meat products, and milk, it was not the company's major item. And when the National Biscuit Company took Bennett Biscuit Company over in 1931, it wasn't with the intention of cornering the dog-biscuit market. As it turned out, however, everything in Bennett's line went to the dogs *except* the dog biscuit. Nabisco originally sold Milk-Bone as "a dog's dessert" and "a nourishing snack for canines." But Milk-Bone made it big when it was discovered to be a deliverance from doggy breath. That's something that even real bones can't offer.

The Cigarette Hawk Speedboat

The Cigarette is long and slender, but that's not why it got its name. Cocaine smugglers use a Cigarette once and then throw it away—a $105,000-plus nondeductible operating expense—but that's not how it got its name either. The name, according to Don Aronow, who designed and built the first Cigarette in

able to hit more than 70 mph with fierce nonchalance, the Cigarette speedboat, is all speedboat, and nothing but speedboat, a bathtub toy of the gods with no room for sunbathing or sipping piña coladas. Despite sophisticated hull design and ingenious applications of exotic plastics, the Cigarette is about as basic as a boat can be; other than the occasional illicit import run, its purpose is almost childishly simple—to make grown men fly. Some of the grown men who own the thousand or so Cigarettes now in use are King Hussein of Jordan, King Juan Carlos of Spain, knave Robert Vesco of the Caribbean, and citizen George Bush of the Potomac. And, fighting fire with their own smoke, the U.S. Coast Guard.

1969 and proceeded to win nine of the eleven races he entered that year, originally belonged to a notorious and uncatchable Prohibition rumrunner in the Sheepshead Bay area of New York. □
There are no frills on the Cigarette Hawk. Thirty-eight feet long, powered with twin Hawk 500 engines,

Silly Putty Toy

What's in a name? In the case of Silly Putty, absolutely everything. It is both silly and putty and endlessly wondrous. You can stretch it like taffy, you can use it to pick up an image from a comic book and then pull the image into a funny contortion. You can knead it. You can mold it. You can bounce it—and high,

too (it has a rebound capacity 25 percent greater than a rubber ball's). You can even shatter it with a sharp blow from a hammer. Pretty good so far. But the most delightful (because most unexpected) quality it has is that it cleaves. With just a snap of the wrists you can break it in half, leaving you with two even and smooth edges.

Everyone has a favorite way to play with Silly Putty, and the Binney and Smith promotional copy suggests some useful purposes as well, like using it to stabilize a teetering table, clean typewriter keys, or remove lint. But surely, absolute *uselessness* is its true essence.

This was the very quality that made Silly Putty a significant but puzzling scientific invention whose time would never come. In the early forties the War Production Board was desperately in

need of a synthetic rubber, and they proposed to a number of major companies that silicone might hold the secret. A General Electric engineer named James Wright, in the course of making a point to some of his cohorts, tossed a handful of boric acid into some silicone oil. To Wright's surprise and satisfaction, the two elements polymerized. He exuberantly picked up the gray substance and threw it to the floor. To everyone's amazement, it bounced. No question, he had created something here. But what? In fact, no one ever took out a patent on what came to be known in the scientific community as bouncing putty, since no one knew any practical use for it.

In 1945, GE sent samples to many of the world's top engineers—with no results. It took a marketing man, Peter Hodgson, to see that the queer stuff was clearly a toy. So he packaged it in plastic eggs (another inspiration) and sold it for a dollar. If you need an antidote for a world in which everything does something, just get yourself some wonderful bouncy, stretchy, shattery, indestructible, miracle superuseless, and inimitable Silly Putty.

Crayola Crayons

A Crayola crayon box—its reassuring and familiar yellow and green cardboard promising nontoxic delight—is something to which almost any grown-up can be counted on to respond with fondness. Crayolas are part of everyone's childhood. The colors are vivid and *right*. The red is real red—not too

orangy or pinky purpley. Just *red*. The green is green. No subtle khaki or pine hue. The brown is perfect for hair or trees, the yellow sunny, the purple fit for a king's robe. And the orange almost edible. You can make the colors soft by using them lightly on their sides. Or you can make them dark and heavy, with none of those pallid waxy streaks some other crayons make. What a treat to fold back the lid on the brand new box of Crayolas and see every single color lined up at attention with a perfect point.

Crayolas are made from four ingredients: pigment, paraffin, paper, and stearic acid—which is a meat by-product. So, strange as it may seem, the cost of a box of Crayolas can fluctuate with the price of a hamburger. The enchanted name Crayola comes from a combination of the words *crayon* and *olea*—the latter comes from *oleaginous*, meaning oily. Crayolas were given their name by Alice Binney, a grade-school teacher who was the wife of Edwin Binney. It was Edwin (at the prompting of Alice) who first came up with the formula for the crayons. And it was Edwin who first came up with the idea of boxing the color sticks in sets of 8, 16, and 24. Of course, in this endlessly perfectable world, it is now possible to get Crayolas in giant-size boxes of 64 (an intimidating concept), and jumbo-size crayons, and even—if you can imagine holding such a thing in your hand—anti-roll Crayolas with one flat side. However you take your crayons, in all their brilliant splendor, Crayolas are still among the cheapest and most satisfying investments money can buy.

Please read Crayola crayons wherever Crayola appears. Crayola is a registered trademark of Binney & Smith Inc.

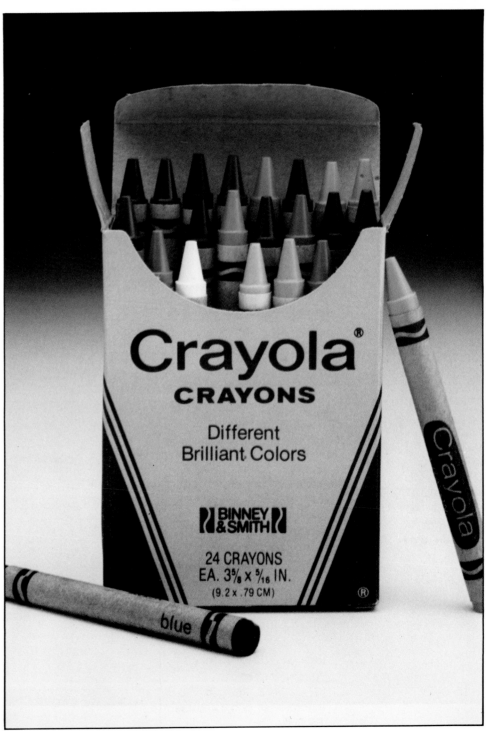

Crayola® CRAYONS

Different Brilliant Colors

BINNEY & SMITH

24 CRAYONS
EA. 3⅝ x 5⁄16 IN.
(9.2 x .79 CM)

The Harley-Davidson ElectraGlide Motorcycle

An engineer will tell you that two cylinders don't make sense anymore. A performance freak will tell you that the imports can eat it up. Don't argue; they probably wouldn't understand that on the shimmering blacktop of the id, every man rides a Harley.   ☐ More than seventy years ago, William Harley and three Davidson

have been added—overhead valves came in with the 1941 "knucklehead," hydraulic forks and an electric starter appeared in the fifties and sixties (all of which did nothing to lighten the mood of the dour highway patrolmen who ride these battle chargers). But even with its limousine ride and middle-American stolidity, the ElectraGlide still retains its primal élan; blasting by at full bore, it sounds just like a dinosaur gargling.

brothers turned out their first V-twin, 61-cubic-inch dream machine, establishing a basic design pattern that has never changed. By 1922, the 74-inch JD model had emerged from their Milwaukee shop and created the line currently embodied by the massive 80-inch ElectraGlide.   ☐ Along the way certain amenities

The Zippo Lighter

In a dispirited world of dull, charmlessly efficient butane sticks hissing at the cigarettes of conscience-stricken smokers, the beautiful, basic Zippo Model 200 is an unashamed feast for the senses, as good and generous a machine as any America has produced. From the unmistakable *kerchung* of its lid

being opened, to the heady aroma of the fuel vapors trapped underneath, to the soft blue and yellow billow of its flame, the Zippo is a flawless blend of art and utility.

Though the clean lines of the Zippo might easily have sprung from the mind of a Mies van der Rohe, its creator was, in fact, George G. Blaisdell, co-owner of the Blaisdell Oil Company in Bradford, Pennsylvania, who in 1932 redesigned an Austrian army lighter and brought smoking into the modern age. Blaisdell believed so emphatically in his product that he promised to repair any Zippo—damaged in any way, no questions asked—free of charge. The offer still goes, with the result that almost half a million lighters come back to Bradford every year for restoration, and they are invariably turned around within forty-eight hours.

When it comes to evocative power, the Zippo has no equal. Fire one up in a high wind to light a crackling Camel and you can dream anything you want: Tobruk, bomber command, the Mermansk run, Bogie's lip, Ingrid's eyes . . .

The Cartier Santos Watch

In 1904, the dashing Brazilian aviator Alberto Santos-Dumont, inventor of an ovoid-shaped gas-filled airship with which he was beating all comers in European air races, complained to his Parisian friend Louis Cartier that it was a nuisance to reach for his pocket watch while keeping his balloon on course. A

few months later, Cartier solved the problem in his characteristically elegant manner and presented Santos-Dumont with a miniature watch on a leather strap that buckled around the wrist. Whether or not this was the first time anyone put a watch on the wrist is arguable, but the Santos very likely is the first watch expressly designed for the purpose. And surely no watch since has done more for the wrists it has adorned.

The Santos is everything the mystical term "timepiece" implies. Its sculpted case and sober Roman numerals suit the seriousness of its purpose, nothing less than the measurement of the thread of our lives. The circular movement of its gunmetal-blue hands symbolizes the nature of time itself, and the lack of a second hand lets us forget how quickly the minutes pass. True to its maker's original design, the Santos is neither self-winding nor quartz-powered, so that it needs us as much as we need it. The Santos is not nearly as trendy as its cousin, the Cartier Tank watch. But if time is of the essence, this is the essence of time. A votre Santos!

Coppertone Suntan Lotion

The magic potion that turns you brown instead of red was the solid-gold idea of a Dr. Green—Ben Green, to be precise—who in 1944 formulated a protective lotion for airmen who had to bail out over the Pacific. His formula replaced the standard issue amber petrolatum, known universally as axle

suntan lotion in the world. But since there are all manner of tanning lotions between Dr. Green's elixir and axle grease (a mix of baby oil and iodine is the traditional incendiary balm for young sunbathers), why Coppertone? The answer is simple and has little to do with sun protection: It's the smell, that wonderful, heady aroma that instantly evokes the best of times. It's the conch shell of lotions: Put a bottle of Coppertone to your nose and you can hear the ocean. The brewers of the glorious stuff claim that the smell is mainly the essence of night-blooming jasmine, but mixed in there too, surely, is a secret extract of hot sand, salt water, endless summer days, and the hyperactive glands of teenagers.

grease. There are better ways to get a tan than being shot down, of course, so after the war Dr. Green dedicated his Coppertone to the browning of America with the slogan "Don't Be a Paleface." ☐ In 1957 he sold his company to Plow, Inc., in Memphis, Tennessee, and today Coppertone is the top-selling

The Goodyear Blimp

There are two aerial events that nearly everyone will look up for: to see what the skywriting will say and to watch the Goodyear Blimp move with elephantine grace across the sky. The large gray bomb-shaped blimp is at once a rare and familiar sight, always unexpected and always wondrous. Even

grayness. They are both magical and surreal, with a benign eeriness that engenders no fear, even in young children. There are, in fact, only four blimps flying today—one (the *Europa*) in Europe, and the other three in the United States, the *America*, based in Houston; the *Enterprise,* based in Pompano Beach; and the *Columbia*, based in Los Angeles. (In case you didn't catch on, Goodyear names its blimps for America's Cup winners.)

Here are some basic facts about blimps: They have a cruising speed of 35 mph and a maximum speed of 50 mph. They fly at an altitude of between 1,000 and 3,000 feet (although they can go as high as 10,000 feet). They can operate eight hours a day for almost a week on the amount of fuel a jumbo jet uses to taxi from the ramp to the runway. And contrary to

what your dictionary says, they're called blimps because that's the sound an airship makes when you plunk its body with a flip of your thumb. Honest. Blimps may look like the simplest of vehicles, but like major talents they travel with a considerable entourage. Each blimp has five pilots, sixteen crewmen, and its own PR man. In addition, each one has four ground support vehicles—a sedan, a passenger van (six by-invitation-only guests can go along for the ride), a tractor trailer rig that serves as a mobile maintenance facility, and a specially designed bus that functions as the flight center. The *Hindenburg* gave blimps a bad name, but in fact they've been flying safely since 1917.

Blimps belong to a world long past, when distance was related to time, when to travel to a faraway land meant to move across sky or sea or land at a pace that conveyed a feeling of the many miles journeyed. Travel was romantic then, and to spot a blimp floating above is to return, for a moment, to that pre-Mach world gone by.

when you know what keeps it up (202,700 cubic feet of nonflammable helium), it's still an incomprehensible sight, a nonthreatening behemoth, floating slowly, ever so slowly, from unknown places toward unknown destinations. They loom large, these blimps, but there's nothing sinister about their lumbering

The Bean Maine Hunting Boot

There is more than a little of the duckbill platypus in the Bean hunting boot. It's neither one thing nor the other, a griffinlike creature that looks as if it was put together by a committee unable to reach a consensus. But like the platypus, the Bean boot owes the world no apologies; it does just what it's supposed to do

brilliantly well and its odd looks serve as a reminder that beauty is on the foot of the beholder. The rubber and leather crossbreed—now a must item in every urban plowboy's wardrobe and much copied by other shoe companies—is both historically and philosophically the wellspring of L.L. Bean's growth into Maine's Mecca.

Before the boot came along the only Bean's up there was the Ervin Bean haberdashery in Freeport, where Erv's younger brother Leon Leonwood Bean worked selling shirts and overalls. Life might have been beautiful for Leon if only he'd been able to find just the right boot for his hunting trips—all-rubber was too cold, and all-leather cracked and leaked. So around 1910, with straight-ahead New England logic, L.L. Bean designed a boot with a rubber overshoe bottom and a leather upper. His curious invention kept Bean's feet dry and felt good, so he had a local cobbler make up a hundred pairs and sold them through a mailing list of hunting-license holders. Ninety pairs of the first batch came apart, so Bean borrowed money, paid out refunds, and enlisted the help of U.S. Rubber to come up with a new prototype. It worked, and it still does. Suburban style may be overrunning the Bean catalogue like a plague of crabgrass, but the hunting boot prevails, perfect, uncompromised, and unimprovable. And odd. Like the Platypus.

Green Giant Peas

There really is a Valley of the Jolly Green Giant. It's the Minnesota Valley, and it was first explored by a Frenchman named Pierre Charles Le Seuer—as in the peas. When the Minnesota Valley Company was founded in 1903 it was specifically created to can cream-style corn, but in 1907 the company decided

to can peas, too. At the time the most popular kind of peas were early June peas, which were tiny, smooth, and round. But the company wanted to pack an even sweeter English garden variety that were big, wrinkled, and oblong. Needless to say, this "Prince of Wales" pea was about as popular as Wallis Warfield Simpson.

The company, unable to sell the new peas to any of their private label customers, decided to market them under their own label as "Green Giant peas." But the designation green giant was descriptive and therefore unpatentable. Enter the

Green Giant himself, designed as a symbol for the can and therefore a patentable personage. That original Green Giant, who first appeared in 1925, was actually a sullen, white dwarf in a bearskin. It took the genius of Leo Burnett to transform him into the Jolly Green Giant we all know and love.

One of the very best things about these bigger than pea-size peas—besides the fact that they're easier to gather on your fork—is that there isn't a clunker in the mouthful. All imperfectly flavored peas are eliminated by a simple method the company came upon in 1933. Apparently tender peas float and mature (read "tasteless") peas sink. Also, Green Giant peas *are* "Picked at the fleeting moment of perfection," and this is measured by a Tenderometer, a machine which registers the force required to cut through a pea. And whenever the Tenderometer indicates that a particular planting is at the perfect point, the peas are summarily harvested and, within three hours, packed in their jolly green cans. This is why every last one of them is so sweet and tender. More peas, please.

The Frisbee Flying Saucer

If the thermonuclear bomb is the most significant invention of this all-too-significant century, the Frisbee flying saucer has a legitimate claim to being the most perfect. Simple and beautiful at rest, the plastic disc is as pure and graceful in action as anything man has ever conceived. An overly serious mind

might conjure up Jungian thoughts of religious symbolism—mandalas, sun discs, and all that. But the Great Truth of the Frisbee is simply that its function is pure pleasure.

The Manhattan Project that produced this elegant technology was a Californian named Walter Frederick Morrison, who, the story goes, added to his income in the mid-fifties by selling "invisible wire" at carnivals. Morrison demonstrated the nonexistent wire by tossing a metal pie tin in the air and appearing to guide its flight. Morrison soon switched to a plastic disc for safety's sake.

The Wham-O Company of San Gabriel, California, licensed the disc (not the wire) and produced, over the next several years, the Pluto Platter, the Sailing Satellite, the Sputnik, the Flying Saucer, and finally, the numinous, unencumbered, impeccable Frisbee flying saucer. Though the company now markets various weights and sizes, the regular nine-inch model is all you really need. Almost anywhere on a summer's day, Frisbees are ubiquitous. Since that first fateful day in 1957 when Mr. Morrison and Wham-O pledged their troth, the Frisbee has been the undisputable small wonder of our less-than-wonderful technological age.

The English Bull Terrier

It might be argued that *all* dogs, being creatures of nature, are quintessential. But the fact is that thoroughbred dogs aren't natural at all, just another product of man's endlessly energetic, shameless meddling. What a dog may think of as a great time a serious dog owner considers the business of

breeding. And the dizzying spectrum of dogs, from chihuahua to Irish wolfhound, testifies to the instability of the breeder breed. Perhaps if someone had just produced the bull terrier in the first place, we'd have only one kind of dog—the absolutely right kind—and we could get on with the work of breeding better politicians.

As it is, however, the bull terrier didn't appear until around 1835, when some enterprising sport mated an English terrier (a breed now extinct) with a bulldog. It seems possible that the original breeder was a bit taken aback by what he had wrought, because he neglected to take credit for his work. It wasn't long before breeder dissatisfaction crept in, and one of the prototype dogs—known at the time as the bull and terrier—was crossed with a Spanish pointer to gain size. In 1860 breeder James Hinks decided what the world needed was an all-white version, which, with a little help from our best friends, he proceeded to produce. Thus perfected, the bull terrier went on to become the most

fashionable dog of its day in England.

The reason is obvious. The b.t. is the very dog of very dogs, a kind of child's drawing of a dog (or a kid *in* a dog suit). At around fifteen inches high and weighing forty-five pounds or so, with the approximate density of a plaster-of-paris lawn ornament, the b.t. is so undecorated and functional-looking that it might have been designed by Walter Grrropius.

The bull terrier is not a dog for those who wish a pet merely to look elegantly decorative; that's a job for the whippet. The b.t.'s appeal is its appearance of prehistoric ferocity. No spaniel-eyed sniveling for this dog, nothing Lassie-ish and goody four-paws. The bull terrier's function is to fight, though he's perfectly happy not to, and he looks like the meanest regular at a bar you wish you hadn't stepped into (despite the silly smile on *this* one). Just over a thousand bull terriers are registered with the American Kennel Club, a rare few compared to the vast common herd of ninety-five-thousand-plus poodles. Clearly, not everyone is ready for the dog's dog in this frivolous roll-over-and-beg world.

The Louisville Slugger Baseball Bat

The game of baseball has at last proved mortally unfaithful, revealing itself to be more a business than an act of mystical devotion. But the great tool of the trade threatens no such infidelity. Milled from northern white ash by the druids at Hillerich and Bradsby in Jefferson, Indiana, the bat of heroes (from

made in 1884 by John Hillerich, the seventeen-year-old son of a Louisville, Kentucky, churnmaker, when he saw a local baseball hero break his bat in the middle of the game. He offered to make the star a better weapon, and did so that same day, precisely to his first customer's specifications. The bat held, the hitter hit, and orders began to come in for what Hillerich called (after

Louisville's local name) the Falls City Slugger. Happily, Hillerich realized that his bat's name sounded like that of a second-rate palooka and changed it in short order. Although the past decade has brought strong competition in the vulgar form of aluminum bats, Hillerich and Bradsby still produces a million Sluggers a year. What it's selling isn't just the essence of baseball, it's the remembrance of things past, warm in the hands and a sweet-grained delight to the eye. In truth, the difference between driving a double up the left-field line and braining a saber-toothed tiger is less than we might imagine. The Slugger is the impeccably correct instrument for the former and would have served admirably for the latter.

Ruth to Reggie) has a simple brute appeal that is no easier to explain than is the sea-deep satisfaction of hitting a ball over a center fielder's outstretched glove. From its tapered handle to its potent head, the Louisville Slugger is one of the most splendidly tailored devices in all sport.   ☐ The bat was first

Jockey Briefs

It was a long, inconvenient road from the codpiece to the Kenosha Klosed Krotch, an X-shaped overlapping opening incorporated into union suits in 1910 by S.T. Cooper and Sons of Kenosha, Wisconsin. This welcome innovation allowed men minor relief without the necessity of major disrobing. Thank

God Almighty, free at last! But the age of truly modern underwear wasn't yet imminent. Not until after World War I did long underwear lose its dominant popularity, spurned by veterans whose army summer issue had been short shorts. Then in 1934 someone with Cooper Underwear saw an abbreviated swimsuit on the French Riviera and brief Style 1001 was born. This was soon replaced by the more streamlined Style 1007, known today as the Jockey Classic Brief. It's hard to imagine life without Jockey briefs, They seem ancient in their wisdom—soft, white, dependable, with their brand name stitched around the waistband like a news flash in Times Square. Perhaps the ultimate recognition of Jockey's eminence is the fact that one of America's quintessential derivative designers has chosen to market his own version, virtually indistinguishable from the original except for the name on the band (and the price on the tag), a product with all the integrity of the Nashville Parthenon. Out, out, brief Calvin! Onward, Kenosha Klassical Konsciousness!

Monopoly Board Game

Whoever said "Never confuse fantasy with 'realty'" never heard of Charles B. Darrow. In 1934 he brought a game of his invention to Parker Brothers, and they turned him down. But a year later they changed their minds, and Monopoly has been their best-seller ever since. Atlantic City is hardly the most

American of cities, but it has produced two of the most American of concepts—the Miss America Pageant and Monopoly. If a foreigner (Monopoly is published in twenty-eight countries) wants to learn the American theory of business, he has only to master this game. Using a combination of common sense, cunning, diligence, and a basic desire to succeed, especially at someone else's expense, you can win—BIG. But like the American dream itself, it can all be lost by a mere roll of the dice.

What's so great about this game? It's for serious game players and time-passers alike, you can accumulate enviable sums of money, and it can take hours, even days, to play. But best of all, you actually get something for nothing: two hundred dollars just for passing Go.

The Ghurka Express Bag No. 2

The name Ghurka summons up images of antique lands and indomitable soldiers, of lancers and the Regiment, of the thin red line, *Four Feathers,* and the Raj. The Ghurkas were and are soldiers in Her Majesty's service, and a Ghurka bag definitely looks like the kind of thing a loyal soldier of Victoria's vast

empire would carry to the far-flung borders, which is why it is remarkable that they are an American creation of rather recent vintage. First marketed in 1976, they came on the scene with a ready-made classicism, sprung full panoplied from the head of one Marley Hodgson.

Ghurka bags come in all sizes and shapes, some of which betray the newness of Ghurka's history (like the Grip No. 35, for example, which is

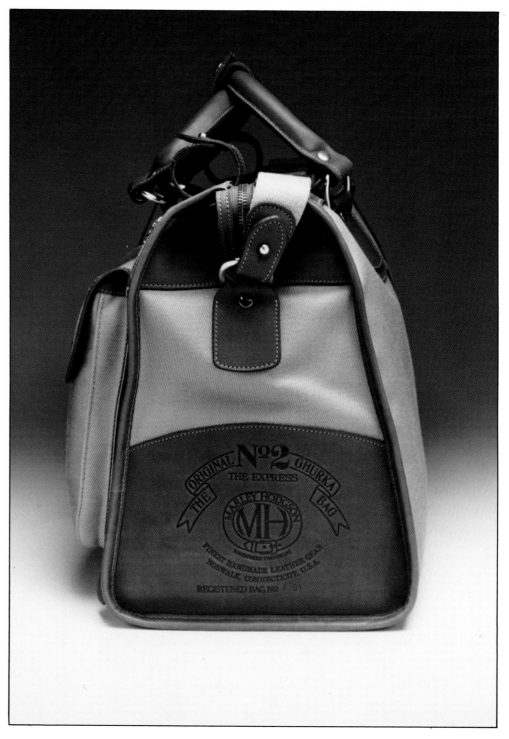

a camera bag). But there are others as timelessly romantic as one would romantically hope they were—like the Express No. 2, the first bag the company made and still the most popular. If Mary Poppins had been a Wren she would have carried such a bag, with its two large pockets and umbrella holder attached to the handles, its shoulder strap and handle, and, for all we know, a compartment just right for a swagger stick. Like many articles that Ghurka makes, the No. 2 comes in twill and leather or all leather. But it's the combination of taupe-colored twill and warm brown leather that makes Ghurka bags look like they've been around since the days of Gunga Din. That twill is tough stuff—industrial strength and reinforced at all stress points. Both the twill and the leather are waterproofed by a process that actually was developed for treating the leather gear of Her Majesty's troops. And each bag is individually numbered and registered, so that you know that yours is distinctive and unique. Pity we lost Indja, what?

The Polaroid SX-70 Camera

Once upon a time there was a faithful Brownie who said, "You push the button and we do the rest." So you pushed the button (or rather, your father pushed it . . . you were trying grimly to keep smiling) and the film was sent off to Kodak, king of the Brownies, in a far northern realm called Rochester. And Kodak

worked some magic and back came pictures of the tops of telephone poles and the lower portions of aunts and cousins and you. And though through the years the Brownies changed, we always waited for the magic to be done in the faroff realm.

Then in 1972 there came new magic, from Dr. Edwin Land, Wizard of Eyes, and his instant elves. It was called the SX-70, ostensibly for the file drawer in which the project was kept (but one might wonder at the potent implications of the

"SX" part). The magic of the SX-70 happened right in your hand, with almost everything except focus automatic and a self-contained film sandwich in which metalized dyes formed the lower portion of you as you watched. King Kodak grew angry and made his own version, but it wasn't the same. No SX appeal. It didn't have, for one thing, the incredible penny arcade whirring noise when the picture burped out.

In 1978 Polaroid decided that focusing was more than its devotees ought to be asked to do. An ultrasonic sending and receiving device was added that beams a millisecond chirp of high-frequency sound toward a subject, collects the echo, and gets a tiny digital computer to figure out the distance and automatically adjusts the focus. Bats have been doing that for eons, of course, but they can't take pictures. After the SX-70, it's hard to imagine what more a camera could do, short of illicit acts. After all, this is the only camera that you can use to photograph your dog, or to call him.

Ray-Ban Sunglasses

They are, to be specific, ultraviolet-light Ray-Bans, and they've been banning the rays for almost half a century. They were developed by Bausch and Lomb at the request of the U.S. Army Air Corps to protect pilots from the dangers of high-altitude glare. And, since the thirties, American fly boys have been

then, as now, as the Large Metal Sunglass (not terribly creative, but certainly descriptive), these aviator glasses have been imitated but never bettered. Well, that's not quite true. Bausch and Lomb has developed a number of sophisticated lenses since, but they still manufacture the original green lens for the diehards. One thing that has changed, probably forever, is the Large Metal frame itself. Once 12-karat gold filled, it's now gold electroplated as a consequence of the soaring price of gold in the seventies. So if you've got a pair of those 12-karat classics, *don't lose them.* You'll never see their like again.

going off into the wild blue yonder wearing them. (During World War II, all Ray-Bans produced went exclusively for military use.) We don't know if that old soldier, General Douglas MacArthur, died with his Ray-Bans on, but they were certainly as much a part of his image as his corncob pipe.   ☐ Known

Budweiser Beer

As any teenage boy can tell you, and as psychologists have spent much time and many grants to find out, a nickname is a good measure of popularity. And with Budweiser's popularity unsurpassed, it's not surprising that the world's favorite beer has come to be known simply and familiarly as "Bud." Sometimes it seems that

this Bud's for everybody on the planet, or how else could it be that more than 55 million barrels of the brew—around 2 billion gallons—are sipped, guzzled, quaffed, or chugged each year. Since brewers Adolphus Busch (who had married into the family of a St. Louis brewery owner named Eberhard Anheuser) and his friend Carl Conrad set out to create the first national beer in 1876, Budweiser, with its "A and eagle" insignia and its comfortingly hectic label, has been the great American beer. Connoisseurs may spurn it—there's none of the snob appeal, bouquet, or palate clout of a Czech pilsner or a Dutch dunkel—but the man who's sure to be having a whole lot more than one is a whole lot more likely to opt for Bud than anything else. We don't need an eight-horse hitch of Clydesdales or TV's Ed MacMahon to tell us that good old Bud, resplendent in red, white, and blue, is *the* beer of the realm.

The Hershey's Chocolate Kiss

The idea of a candy called a kiss—and a candy shaped like a nipple at that—is quite erotic. Hard to imagine that this lovely morsel, so delicately shaped and lovely to suck on, was first introduced in 1907. Kisses are actually an imitation of a candy called a Wilbur Bud (produced since 1884 in a factory in Lititz, Pennsylvania). Wishful imagination notwithstanding, the name of the candy has nothing to do with osculation. If you check your Webster's, you'll find among the definitions for "kiss" this one: "A bite-size piece of candy often wrapped in paper or foil." The plume—like the breath of a kiss—was added in 1921. In an age of vast and complicated gratifications, the Hershey's kiss is a lovely anachronism, delicately shaped and individually gift wrapped. It fits perfectly in your mouth and dissolves warmly into sweet nothingness. The very simplicity of the kiss makes it more elegant than the most costly candy you can buy. To dangle a single kiss before a beloved, to drop it into his hand, or to leave it secretly for him to discover is a romantic gesture both sweet and resonant, which is why the introduction, in 1978, of the giant Hershey's Kiss is so distressing. This supererogated confection is like a long, wet, smothery kiss from an overardent lover. It doesn't let you breathe and you can never react to it as you feel you should. You can have too much of a good thing. The sweet little kiss is perfect.

The Volkswagen Beetle Car

When the first VW, its characteristic beetle shape already defined, was introduced as the "people's car" of Germany in February 1936, the car's lines were perfectly in keeping with the aerodynamic ideas of the age of streamlining. But after the war, when the bugs began to arrive in the United States, the car

was an anomaly, a prophet before its time, that tended to inspire either fierce loyalty or open ridicule. In an age of tail fins, swaths of chrome, and general gargantuanism, it was a *wagen* for some of the *volks,* but definitely not for most. But the car's design, the work of Dr. Ferdinand Porsche, was so extraordinary and unimprovable that in 1981, when the 20 millionth "Beetle" rolled off an assembly line in Mexico, the car differed only in details from Porsche's first 1934 drawings (the essence of purity, the first VWs didn't even have rear windows). During all its years of increasing popularity, no one ever really tried to copy the "Beetle." Incredible!

David Langley

The American Express Card

It's hard to imagine, but before 1958 no one could leave home *with* it because it didn't even exist. But within the first year of its existence, there were 253,000 cardholders. Today, there are some 15 million. There are very few things listed in this book that have improved over the years, but the American Express card is an

exception to the Gold Plate Rule of Modern Life that change is usually for the worse. The card used to be purple, because that was the color of American Express Traveler's Cheques. But in 1969, it took on the decidedly appropriate look of play money. Known as the Money Card, its new green color instantly transformed it into a symbol of all it represents— an imitation material standing in for what may be imitation funds. Like money from a board game, the card is a naïve copy of real money, but that only enhances its quality of "let's pretend."

Considering how many people carry this card, it's interesting to realize how much a feeling of status having one still confers. Not only do you carry one, but so do astronauts, best-selling authors, and vice-presidential candidates. Never mind that all you have to earn is $12,500 a year—who's going to know *that*? In fact, the only seedy thing about the card is the hint of stubble on the centurion's chin, a grim reminder of the reality that awaits at the end of the month. But never mind that. That's *then*. With this little piece of promissory plastic on your person the world is yours *today*.

M&M's Chocolate Candies

M&M's is one candy that doesn't have to pander to extraterrestrials or even Hollywood moguls. It may be forever famous for being the candy that *didn't* melt in E.T.'s mouth. (M&M's didn't choose to get involved in the merchandising of *E.T.*, so E.T. got stuck eating Reese's Pieces instead.) These little lapidary bits of

could carry them into battle, providing a quick pick-me-up but leaving trigger fingers itchy but not sticky. M&M's were the creation of Forrest E. Mars, Sr. (son of Frank C. Mars, creator of the Milky Way, Snickers, and Three Musketeers). Mars and his associate Bruce Murrie (the M and M of M&M) formed their own company on this one candy alone. (M&M's peanut version didn't come along until 1954.) But M&M's were so unlike any other candy that their popularity was

immediate and everlasting.

M&M's are fun to eat. You can gobble them up, scoopful by scoopful, cracking the many-colored sugar coatings between your teeth with a gratifying crunch. Or you can mete them out, one by one, and suck on them, savoring the hard coating as it slowly yields to the softer, sweeter center within. And M&M's are pretty. Of course, they were ever so much prettier before the red-dye scare. (One can almost hear the little white laboratory mice squeaking their dismay: "They look so pretty and they taste so good, but I'm sure they're killing me.") The red ones faded from the pack on March 10, 1976. But a handful of these multicolored, perfectly shaped ellipsoids are still lovely to behold. And so delicious. Maybe in *E. T. II* . . .

confection, in their rather sober brown bag, are simply the perfect snack, fulfilling the desire for something sweet without leaving you with the guilty feeling that you've overindulged.   ☐ M&M's have been around since 1941. There's a story, perhaps apocryphal, that they were created expressly for the army so that GIs

Bayer Aspirin

When Hippocrates recommended that a patient with a pain chew willow leaves and call him in the morning, he was prescribing an ancient Greek form of aspirin—the bitter bark contains salicin, a cousin of $C_9H_8O_4$, aspirin's main ingredient. No doubt stressful times for Greeks were hard on willows, too. ☐ The

perfectly round, perfectly white five-grain Bayer aspirin tablet, with its brand name forming a none-too-subtle crossword cross, is medicine's equivalent of the communion wafer. In a way we owe this panacea to an Alsatian chemist named Charles Frederick von Gerhardt, who in 1853 managed to synthesize acetylsalicylic acid, a compound of carbon, hydrogen, and oxygen. But von Gerhardt was satisfied just to produce the compound; neither he nor anyone else seems to have known what to do with it, and aspirin (*a* for acetyl, *spir* for the spirea family of salicylate-containing plants, *in* to end the word) remained the drug of nobody's choice for half a century. Not until 1898 did some unremembered saint discover that aspirin relieved arthritic pain and headache, and pharmacists began giving out the white powder in little envelopes.

In 1915 the Bayer Company of New York began to produce aspirin in tablet form (Bayer had been manufacturing the drug as a powder since 1899 and had trademarked the name). After all these years, and who knows how many headaches banished, no one yet knows quite how aspirin does what it does. But for what it does, each year doctors prescribe aspirin 14 million times.

And call them in the morning.

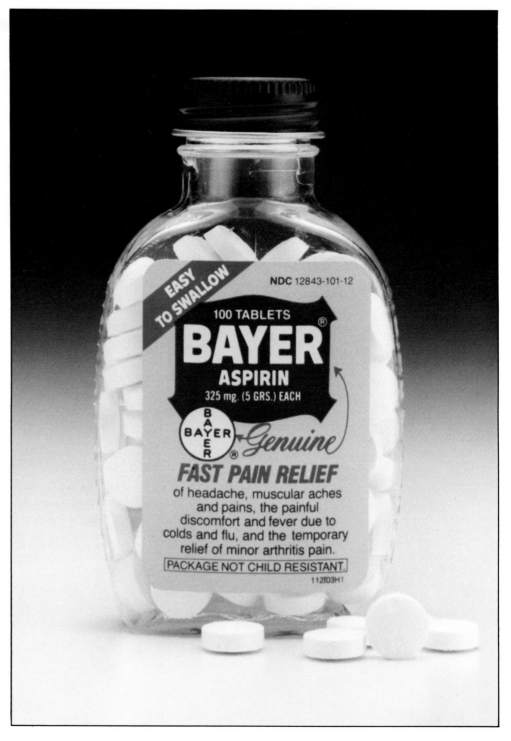

Honey Bear

Who would have thought such a thing possible? Poetry in plastic. And what more perfect evocation of pure satisfaction could there be than a bear filled to the eyebrows with his favorite food, smiling with slightly stunned delight. For this inspired idea we owe an everlasting debt to Ralph Gamber and

Woodrow Miller of the Dutch Gold Honey Company in Lancaster, Pennsylvania. In 1958, when Yogi Bear was hot, Gamber and Miller decided that their honey and the lovable bear were like the material equivalent of onomatopoeia, and they gave the job of creating a properly adorable receptacle to a California company called Olympic Plastics (now, alas, defunct).

Never mind that the bear ended up with six front toes, it couldn't have turned out better, surely one of the greatest packages ever designed. The label even doubles as a bib.

Ever smiling, infinitely user-friendly, the honey bear neatly dispenses a thick strand of honey with a squeeze of its soft, matte-finish belly, then pops right back into shape and sucks in the last drop without letting anything go to waste. The bear is endlessly refillable (and feels 100 percent better full than empty, just like a real bear), but even without honey it does noble service as a bathtub toy, a squirt gun, a classy bud vase, or simply as the objet d'art it is. In its own quiet way, the honey bear demands affection, and, for obvious reasons, it gets what it wants.

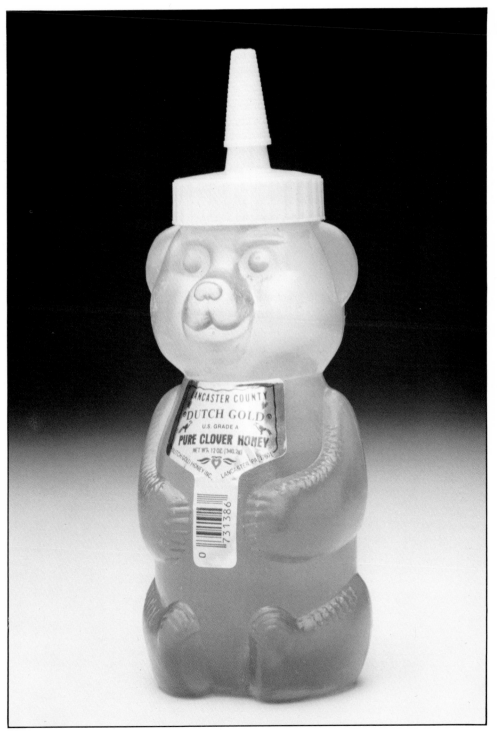

The Faber Mongol #2 Pencil

As common as the pencil may be, to write with anything other than a Mongol #2 is to hamper your creativity. A #3 is too tentative, almost resistant. No matter how heavy the thought, the pencil markings remain faint and unsure. And the #1 pencil is far too soft. The words come out sloppy and smudged. How

clay and graphite. ("Lead pencil" being a complete misnomer, since pencils never have contained any lead.) The more clay in the mixture, the harder and grayer the "lead." The more graphite, the softer and blacker it is.

Mongol's also are topped with the best erasers. You never have to worry about making a smudge worse than the one you started with. And if you're an eraser gnawer, you'll need a pull in excess of five pounds to end up with an eraser in your mouth. The Mongol has been *the* pencil since the time of the California Gold Rush. Eberhard Faber was a pencil maker from Germany who built America's first pencil factory where the UN stands today. There is some debate as to whether Faber named these yellow pencils Mongol

after the Asian tribe or the curry soup, but we tend to favor the former. Painting pencils yellow was Faber's idea and to this day yellow pencils are the standard. (Why yellow is such an ideal color for thought is interesting to contemplate. Yellow legal pads, for example, are far more conducive to serious work than white ones. But we digress.) Mongol pencils get thirteen—count 'em—thirteen coats of yellow paint—which is why they don't chip and splinter during difficult creative pauses. Yes, Mongols are very well made pencils. But while t, ey may be indispensable, they're still expendable, which is as it should be, since a pencil's value lies in you, not in it.

Assuming you ever used one up, you could have drawn a line from New York to Princeton or written about forty-five thousand words. A Mongol #2 can be sharpened seventeen times—leaving you with an unemployment-line-size pencil (writers know about such things). Mongol #2s draw the finest line between possibility and certainty. They are the instrument of the mind's music. Write on!

can you communicate a clear and firm idea with thick words?   ☐ No, it's the #2 that gives flow and permanence to your thoughts, and Faber makes the very best pencil there is. Other brand #2s just don't have the same easy-writing lead—they're either too hard or too soft. The Mongol #2 has the perfect mix of

Fox's U-Bet Chocolate Syrup

Fox's U-Bet is a densely delicious, finger-licking rich-tasting chocolate syrup. Its mission in life is to transform the essential into the desirable, the merely good into the best. For example, it does wonders for plain ice cream or graham crackers. Anything you can consume *with* Fox's U-Bet you could as easily

consume without it—but who would want to?

Which brings us to what's really quintessential—the egg cream. Of course, if you've never heard of an egg cream then you've never heard of Fox's U-Bet. The following is the basic recipe for this New York concoction (which is made with neither egg nor cream): Into an eight-inch glass pour one inch of Fox's U-Bet and one inch of whole milk. Squirt in enough seltzer to fill the glass half up, and stir. (The glass should be held at a beer-pouring tilt throughout.) Then squirt seltzer in until the glass is full and brimming over with a foamy head. Then drink it down immediately. This last is very important. These things fade faster than you can say "Jackie Robinson," and really, there's nothing less delectable than a decomposing egg cream.

You can use whole milk or half & half, or seltzer or club soda, but the choices end

there. Fox's U-Bet is the authenticating and essential ingredient in the true egg cream. Fox's has been enriching egg creams since long before Perrier water replaced seltzer. Just check out the little moppet. No one in the company knows who she is, but her face and her bob date the label to sometime in the twenties. The chocolate syrup itself dates to 1900, the year Herman Fox and his wife, Ida, established H. Fox and Company. Herman deserted the company for a few years to explore oil wells in Texas, but that turned out to be a good thing. When he returned he had added the phrase "You bet!" to his vocabulary.

Since it was copyrighted in 1925, neither the bold yellow label nor the dense chocolate syrup inside have changed. And it's still the pride of the Fox family. But Fox's U-Bet has traveled far from its homely Brooklyn beginnings. Woody Allen uses it. Jerry Lewis loves it. And when the Rolling Stones played Madison Square Garden on their 1981 tour, David Fox was requested to deliver vast quantities of U-Bet backstage. Yessiree, Fox's is the syrup of the stars. You bet!

Lacoste Polo Shirt

First, let's talk nomenclature. What is commonly called the alligator shirt is nothing of the kind. The well-known reptile that hovers over the heart of loyal Lacoste wearers is, in fact, a crocodile, from the nickname of French tennis star Réné Lacoste. Just why Lacoste was called the Crocodile is uncertain, but either his

ferocious game or his elongated nose seems to have been the reason. In 1926 Lacoste broke with the tradition of wearing long-sleeve white broadcloth shirts on the court, showing up instead in a cotton polo shirt with a green croc sewn on the chest. Lacoste retired from tennis in 1929, by which time interest in his shirt had grown. In 1933 Lacoste had formed a company that began turning out the reptilian polo shirts, and they've been doing it ever since.

In 1951 the shirt came to America and went nowhere, until (according to the Republican version of the story) President Eisenhower wore one during one of his well-publicized golf games. Since then the crocodile has never been out of fashion; and if it's become a cliché there are plenty of good reasons, not the least of which is that the tight sleeves make your biceps feel bigger.

Anyone who has ever tried to take off the croc emblem (an operation known as a clichectomy) will know that nothing, absolutely nothing, is so fiendishly well connected. If only airplanes were constructed like that. The surgery takes hours, blurs the eye and dulls the mind, and almost always results in a tiny, telltale hole.

So give the croc his due. Everybody tries to copy it, but the replicas are never as good. And if you have to appear in the same shirt as a million or so bozos, take comfort in the fact that not even Arnold Schwarzenegger looks better in it than you do.

Steiff Teddy Bears

In *Animal Farm* we learned that all animals are equal, but some animals are more equal than others. And this certainly applies to the teddy bear species. Steiff teddy bears are more equal. They're the ones with the movable arms and legs (the first stuffed toy made with moving joints) and the dignified

expression and the solidity of a sandbag. This bear sits up and listens to you earnestly when you talk to it, and it can even sit through long tea parties without drooping. To have a teddy bear such as this as a kid is to learn an early lesson in the nature of the real thing.

These baby-size bears come from Geingen-on-the-Brenz, Germany, a toy-making village of cobblestone streets and gingerbread houses. The original Mama Bear was Margarete Steiff, a dressmaker whose first noncouture creation was an elephant-shaped pin cushion. It was her nephew, Richard, an art student, who around the turn of the century designed the famous bear from sketches he had made of some cubs at the Stuttgart zoo. But back then it was just a Steiff bear, not yet a teddy bear. That name is a purely American invention.

Neither saccharine nor sentimental, Steiffs gain gentleness and vulnerability with age. Like a well-worn pair of slippers or a battered fedora, these bears of our childhood acquire a comfortable dilapidation, giving each of them a personality all its own and making *your* teddy unlike any other bear in the world.

Johnson's Baby Powder

Even on the hottest, stickiest summer's day, a few hearty shakes of Johnson's Baby Powder can make you feel reborn. It slides over your skin to create the finest layer of coolness between you and the crushing air. Johnson's has been "keeping our cool" since 1893. Originally a give-away item, it was included in Simpson's

Maternity Packets for midwives to use on the brand-new baby. And, in fact, the powder itself smells brand new. Like the smell a new doll sometimes has, it's sweet, but not cloying—nothing of maiden aunts and antimacassars. Just sniffing some can soothe a sulky mood.

Maybe we all love Johnson's Baby Powder because it shakes out a memory of total contentment, of a time when our every comfort was attended to by kind and loving hands. Or maybe it's because we associate its pure and innocent smell with the purity and innocence that babyness means. Like apple pie and motherhood itself, it's all-American, which is why it's fitting that the man responsible for the powder's development and marketing was Fred Barnett Kilmer, Johnson and Johnson's first director of scientific laboratories and the father of the poet Joyce Kilmer. Only God can make a tree, but only Johnson's can make a perfect baby powder.

The Swiss Army Knife

It must be one of the most stirring sights imaginable: a platoon of Swiss infantry, each fully trained in long- and short-term finance, crouched at the base of an Alpine slope, waiting to advance against the enemy at the command "Fix scissors!" Or corkscrew. Or screwdriver, bottle opener. Or tweezer, toothpick,

useful pocket knives made by Victorinox and/or Wenger, both purveyors to Alpine warriors for over sixty years. If you can't do it with a Swiss army knife, you probably need a cruise missile. The basic model, pictured here, is relatively austere with only six tools (the Champion weighs in with eighteen, including a Phillips screwdriver and the indispensable wire stripper), but you can still uncork a bottle of claret, slice the truffles, open the caviar, pry the lid off the box of Kron chocolates, and ream out your pipe. And, of course, defend Geneva to the last man.

file, reamer, ruler, fishscaler, dehooker, saw, magnifying glass. For canton and country, lads, charge the hill! With our Swiss army knives, there's no stopping us now!   ☐ After Swiss cheese, numbered Swiss bank accounts, and Swiss chocolate, there's probably nothing quite so famously Swiss as the madly

Levi's Jeans

Their motto is Quality Never Goes Out of Style—and they never have. They've been manufacturing the "501," nearly unchanged, for more than 127 years. The orange-double-arc design on the back pockets is more hallowed than the golden arches of McDonald's—and is the oldest apparel trademark in

continuous use in America. Levi's, unlike most designer items, are known by the designer's *first* name. Levi Strauss, supplied with canvas for tents and covered wagons, went west with the Gold Rush to open an outlet of his family's dry goods business. A born entrepreneur, he soon realized that sturdy pants were what the miners really needed. The canvas was soon replaced by *serge de Nîmes* (a.k.a. denim), a tough cotton fabric he imported from Nîmes, France. The last major design change came in 1873, when copper rivets were added to reinforce the pockets. The idea of jumping into the shower with your Levi's and then letting them dry on your body is as old as Levi's themselves. Except, back then, the cowboys jumped into watering troughs instead. And in this Sanforized, Stay-Press, colorfast world, isn't it comforting that you can still buy something that's *guaranteed* to shrink, wrinkle, and fade?

Bass Weejun Loafers

The much-imitated, never-quite-equaled loafer, an indispensable part of the preppie escutcheon, was first adapted from a Norwegian design (hence the name "weejun") in 1936, and by the late forties was established among the *cognoscenti* as the unapproachably right shoe for casual elegance. For true

believers, an outfit for which Weejuns were not appropriate was simply not worth being seen in. (A friend recalls that as a boy back in 1950 he would agree to play Knights of the Round Table only on the condition that he could pretend that Weejuns had been invented by then.) For the ultimate Weejunite wearing his loafers without socks in the late fall is akin to a yogi's dip in the Ganges, just cooler and cleaner.

The design of the Weejun is little changed since the 1936 version first appeared. Every pair is still hand-stitched, and each pair still has the friendly habit of taking on the separate personality of each foot. After only a month of wearing, the right shoe inevitably looks noticeably different from the left (unless your feet are exactly the same, which they aren't). Alas, the Weejun also retains a heartbreaking tendency to keep getting better right up until the day they fall apart.

The Hamilton Beach Model 936 Drink Mixer

You want a malted? A *real* malted—ice cold and frothy and so thick it can't be sucked through a straw? Well, then you'll just have to invest in a Hamilton Beach 936, the commercial model. Expensive, but worth every one of its more than two hundred dollars. Because *nothing* makes a malted the way

this baby does. It whips up the milk and the ice cream and the syrup with an activator that rotates at an incredible 13,000 (and that's on slow) to 18,000 rpms. The 936 has been much modernized since it was introduced in 1911, but the soul of the old and the new machine is still that wonderful metal container that holds the shake. The best part of having a malted in a candy store was always the extra half a glass or more that remained after your first glass had been filled to the top. The counterman would place it beside your glass and you'd pull at the malted through the straw, all the while keeping your eye on that container, watching the

condensation form on its metal sides, savoring the thought that even when you were finished *there was still more!*

We owe all that joy to Chester Beach (his partner, L. H. Hamilton, was the money man), who developed the world's first fractional horsepower universal motor (which is to say, a motor that ran on both AC and DC power). The first appliance to utilize this revolutionary motor was the milk-shake maker, designed specifically to be used with a newly popular health drink called Horlick's Malted Milk powder. And pretty much the same motor still transforms Horlick's or any other powder or syrup into the thickest, richest, most glorious concoction on this earth.

There's an old joke about a genie who appears behind a luncheonette counter and grants the customer standing before him any wish. "Make me a malted," says the customer. "Poof, you're a malted," says the genie. You can tell if he's a genuine genie if he turns the customer into a malted made in a Hamilton Beach 936.

Coca-Cola Soft Drink

"Coke is it!" No question. In one of the few trademark cases ever reviewed by the Supreme Court, Justice Oliver Wendell Holmes upheld the Coca-Cola trademark, stating, "The name now characterizes a beverage to be had at almost any soda fountain. It means a single thing coming from a single

source and well known to the community." Since that opinion in 1920, the community has expanded to 155 countries. That's because things most definitely do go better with Coke.

The miracle of Coke began in a brass pot in a backyard in Atlanta, Georgia, on a May day in 1886, when a pharmacist named Dr. John Styth Pemberton brewed a distinctive, experimental syrup. He then took the potful to Jacob's Pharmacy where it was combined with soda water and sold for a nickel a glass. Pemberton's partner, Frank M. Robinson, contributed the name (based, some claim, on a dash of cocaine) and the flowing Spencerian script of the logo. And then, having set themselves on the path to greatness, the two sold out.

One Asa G. Chandler knew a pause that paid off when he tasted it, and he bought up all the rights to Coke for a mere $2,300. Chandler not only knew a good thing, he knew how to exploit it. Under Asa's direction, Coke became the most popular drink in the world.

If, like some, you're delighted by incalculable and unfathomable statistics, then you'll want to know that if all the Coke ever produced were poured in 6-1/2-ounce bottles and they were laid end to end, they could go to the moon *and* back 1,045 times. (Who thinks these things up?) The sheer, astounding fact is that 260 million glasses of Coke are gulped down every day, because nothing works like Coke does. Not even water.

And not only does it taste wonderful but it still occasionally can be sipped from those wonderful bottles and glasses. The hobbleskirt green glass bottle was designed in 1916 by the Root Glass Company of Terre Haute, Indiana, and the graceful fountain glass with its flowing white script appeared in 1919. No question—Coke *is* the Real Thing. Coke is it!

Ohio Blue Tip Kitchen Matches

In the everlasting quest for fire, man has used everything from fortuitous lightning to lasers. But the wooden match, following somewhat after the tinderbox and preceding by a long while the butane lighter, is technologically and aesthetically about as perfect a device for creating a flame as can

than others. Alas, such is not the case; the great idea has suffered much in some of its many translations. Paper matches, for the most part, are so insubstantial that the process of lighting them is done quickly and not without some hazard. "Decorator" wooden matches, with gold tips and reedy little sticks, snap as often as they light and burn up at an alarming rate. But Ohio Blue Tips set out to do the job, and they do it, one is tempted to say, matchlessly. Two and three sixteenths of an inch of solid integrity, the Blue Tip will burn for twenty-eight seconds before it burns its user, and it's suitable for chewing even if you don't light it at all.

Why the Blue Tip when there are so many others? England's Swan Vestas are far more fashionable and Diamond Kitchen matches from Springfield, Massachusetts, burn just as brightly. Perhaps the advantage for the Blue Tip is in the poetic irony of heat and flame bursting from that beautiful sky blue, sea blue, cool blue tip. One is tempted to say, striking.

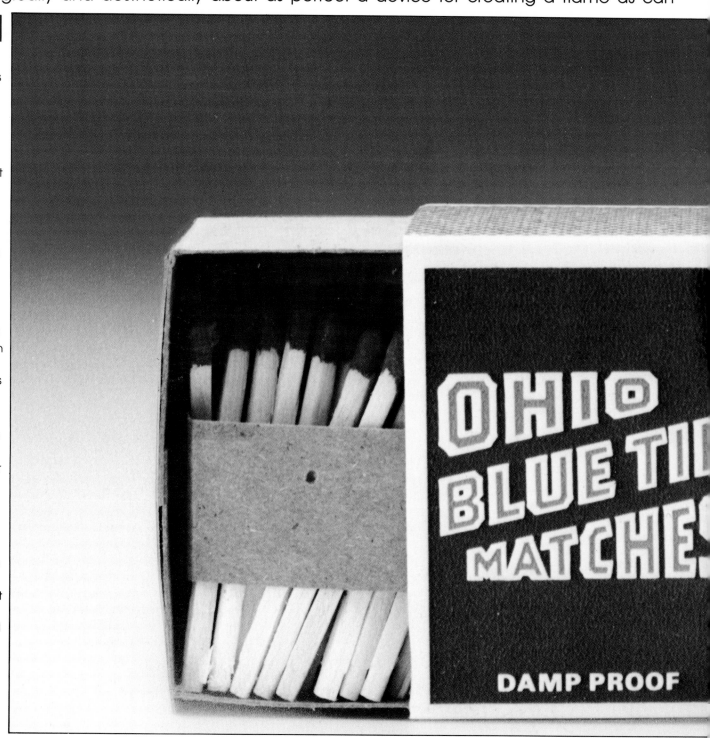

be imagined. To see heat and light explode from the tip of a match at the slightest friction on an abrasive strip is to understand many things about evolution, including why human beings smoke and baboons don't.　　□ It might be thought that there are no bad matches, that some are simply better

Kleenex Tissues

At 8.25 by 9.42 inches, the humble Kleenex is the full measure of our sociotechnological advancement. So deeply a part of our lives is Kleenex, so indubitably the ultimate standard in great American nasal architecture, that its competitors are in the unenviable position of copying it without finding any way to improve

upon it. The next step up is a square of good cotton, and that means a lumpy pocket and life at the Laundromat, endlessly recycling. One of the best things about Kleenex is that in our lamentable use-up-and-throw-away era it is one of the few things we can dispose of with relief instead of guilt.

In the past several years, Kimberly-Clark, the company that introduced Kleenex to a sniveling planet in 1924, has largely abandoned the noble simplicity of their classic blue and white box in favor of relentless bouquets of forced blooms that seem quite capable of inducing allergic reactions all by themselves. But the Pocket Pack, faithful hip flask of the ambulatory cold sufferer, still proudly flies the old school colors. Bless you!

Barnum's Animal Crackers

In the Land of Trivia, knowing the names of Santa's reindeer is definitely a shibboleth of admission. But who among us can name all of Barnum's Animal Crackers? And even if you could, would you know that there are seventeen different animals but eighteen different shapes? They are (in animabetical order): bear,

bison, camel, (Bactrian), cougar, elephant, giraffe, gorilla, hippopotamus, hyena, kangaroo, lion, monkey, rhinoceros, seal, sheep, tiger, zebra. The secret shape is a second bear—one walks, one sits. Although each box contains between twenty and twenty-two cookies, they're dump-packed, which means you could end up with a caravan of camels or a sloth of bears. The other problem, of course, is that many emerge limbless. These cookie shards must *always* be eaten first. Then the animals that remain can be eaten in any number of ways: all duplicates first, all mean ones first, all endangered species last.

The wonderful box with its cutout clown and wheels is a treasure in itself. It even has a string handle so you can carry it along to your friend's house or hang it on your Christmas tree, which was the original purpose for which animal crackers were designed in 1902. But Barnum's Animal Crackers have never been advertised. Apparently, some things in life are just *so* right that we don't even have to be told we need them. On Zebra, on Bison, on Tiger and Cougar . . .

The Märklin Electric HO Gauge Model Trains

The one absolute for sure guaranteed-to-attract-attention window display is a model train, chugging along through pristine green fields dotted with tiny houses, passing over bridges and under tunnels, waiting for railroad signals to flash green, stopping at station houses, running around and around and around

things of the past (with the exception of that traveling museum, the *Orient Express*). Model trains today are being bought for and played with by children who have no idea what train travel is. No matter. These miniature cars traveling within clearly delimited terrains reach into the imagination and draw out our fantasies and dreams of far places.

The only model trains still made that capture the wondrousness of precise

replication are made by Märklin. Märklin trains are manufactured, as they have been since 1891, in Göppingen, West Germany. Costs being what they are these days, only the locomotives are made of metal (die-cast zinc). All of the other cars are made of plastic, but their detailing is exact, and many of the cars can be lit from within. Most of the models are based on European railways, both modern and historical, including catanary (overhead) trains, that can run either on or off cables. Directing these Lilliputian trains over landscapes of your own design is an endlessly rapturous experience. It brings out the little boy in all of us. Even if you're a big girl.

tracks leading nowhere and everywhere. Who can pass by such a wonder and not be caught in its spell?   ☐ The sad fact is, they just don't make model trains the way they used to. But then, they don't make real trains the way they used to either. The luxuriousness and eventfulness of train travel are definitely

The Stetson Hat

The category is: "Hats" for fifty dollars. "He invented the cowboy hat." "Who is John B. Stetson?" The son of a hatmaker from Orange, New Jersey, Stetson went West as a young man to try to build his frail health. It was somewhere along the trail to Pikes Peak that he made himself the very first Stetson. He did it by the

age-old process of "felting." He shaved the fur from rabbit and beaver skins, wet it, dipped it into boiling water and then shaped it into the distinctive high-crowned, wide-brimmed style. That original creation was sold along the way for a five-dollar gold piece, and it wasn't until years later, when he was already a successful hat manufacturer in Philadelphia, that he revived the idea. He gave it the colorful name "Boss of the Plains," sent a sample off to every haberdasher in the West, and soon became a tent-hold name—and a nonsexist one, too. Buffalo Bill and Custer and Tom Mix all wore Stetsons but so did Calamity Jane and Annie Oakley. Many a drugstore cowboy may sport a Stetson for reasons of fashion, but to the *real* cowboy it was more than just a hat. When he wasn't wearing it to protect him from the elements, he could use it to whip a steer, to fan a fire, and to rest his head on at night. And as for its being a ten-gallon hat, well, it *does* hold water and was frequently used that way to relieve a thirsty horse.

Inside each Stetson is a label, and on each label are Xs, sometimes as few as three (though never fewer) and sometimes as many as twenty. What the Xs signify is the proportion of plain old rabbit fur in the felt to more desirable beaver fur. A twenty X Stetson is very like wearing a whole beaver on your head, and if you're only sporting a rabbity three Xs, it's best to keep it under your hat.

Heinz Ketchup

Any way you spell it—catsup, catchup, or ketchup—it's Heinz all the way. There is no other. No blindfold tests necessary. Nothing else pours right, spreads out as reluctantly, or tastes as rich. It may not be possible for ketchup to be too thick, but all other ketchups are just too thin. And they *taste* too thin, too.

For many people a hamburger is merely a vehicle for ketchup, and for those people the disappointment of being confronted by any other brand is enough to make them order a BLT instead. There are two distinctive features of Heinz ketchup—flavor and viscosity. And viscosity is what the company seems to pride itself on most. So much so that they test the stuff with a patented "quantifier"—a laboratory instrument that measures the ketchup's slowness. Slow and steady wins the market. As for the taste, the ketchup is made from a basic recipe that Heinz claims hasn't changed since it was first produced in 1876. Heinz agronomists have even developed their own tomato varieties.

But Heinz ketchup is more than just the ketchup. It's also the bottle. Heinz ketchup is sold in bottles of various sizes and shapes, but the 14-ounce regular is the classic, with the same octagon shape it has had since the turn of the century. It has the fluid modern lines of an Art Deco *objet,* but its shape is eminently practical as well. Those eight sides make it easy to hold on to during that endless wait while the ketchup regally makes its way onto your burger.

In homes of gloved servants and ornate silver settings, the ketchup is decanted into small silver bowls and served with tiny silver spoons. But it's a pretense bordering on sacrilege. Heinz ketchup is the container *and* the contained.

HEINZ
ESTD 1869
TOMATO
KETCHUP
NET WT. 14 OZ.—397 GRAMS
HEINZ ⓤ
57 VARIETIES
CK-257-4-74

The Nathan's Famous Hot Dog

There are hot dogs and there are hot dogs, but Nathan's hot dog—the frank sold at the Coney Island emporium, to be exact—is the one and only. Maybe it's the seedy environment and the salt air, the silliness of traveling out there in the first place, all the ticky-tacky signs announcing everything you can

Yankee ingenuity and enterprise in action. Nathan (you don't name a hot dog Nathan for no good reason) Handwerker and his wife, Ida, worked as roll cutters at Feltman's German Beer Gardens, *the* hot dog emporium of Coney Island at that time. (To give credit where it's due, Charles Feltman, a native of Frankfurt, Germany, had originated the idea of a hot dog on a bun in 1867.) Eddie Cantor and Jimmy Durante were also working at Feltman's as singing waiters. They convinced their friend Nathan to open his own hot dog palace and sell his franks for a nickel, half the price of a Feltman frank. So in 1916, on a three-hundred-dollar investment and a special secret spice recipe from Ida (behind every great . . .), Nathan's was born. At first sales were flat, and for a simple reason that the likes of Vuitton, Gucci, Ralph Lauren, et al., understand all too well: If it's that cheap, how good could it be? So Nathan hit upon a variation of the "trucks-parked-outside-the-diner" theory. He hired young men to dress in white cotton jackets and hang around his eatery conspicuously consuming hot dogs. And happily, his customers leaped to the right conclusion at once: If doctors eat them, they must be good. They're not called Nathan's Famous for nothing. They deserve to be.

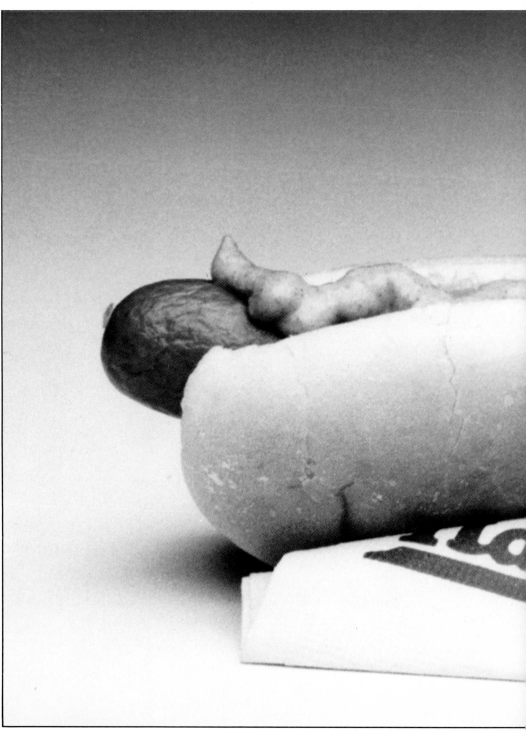

have that *isn't* a hot dog—whatever, no other hot dog has that same crunch to the first bite and satisfying bad-for-you flavor.   ☐ And quite apart from its savory taste, the Nathan's hot dog deserves to be a part of American folklore because its own folklore is so intrinsically American, a case of pure

The Oil Can

Press the button on top of a silicon oil spray can and from the sound it makes you might be doing anything from making your bathroom smell like the Black Forest to spreading something cheesoid on a cracker. But when you use the true oil can there is heard that satisfying *plik-plok, plik-plok* sound that is

like no other, a sound that assures you things are going to be working more smoothly any minute, that the Tin Woodsman will be walking and talking like new. Most of all, it is the sound that indicates the maintenance of civilization as we know it against rust and ruination.

Without the oil can, with its ample domed reservoir and its fit-anywhere spout, the Industrial Revolution might have ground to a stop before it really got rolling. That the impeccably elegant device doesn't appear on the flag of any Western nation (a nice rejoinder to that dour hammer and sickle) is scandalously unfair, as is the fact that its inventor is unremembered, despite the fact that we celebrate the birthday of a man who couldn't tell the difference between America and India.

The version here, made by Eagle Manufacturing Company of West Virginia, faithfully carries on the impeccable design that needs no improvement and that so well symbolizes that battle cry of the well-oiled society: "Can do!"

Now quick, Dorothy, my knees.

LePage's Mucilage

There are glues available these days that enable us to bond together permanently two rhinos with urgent appointments at opposite corners of the Serengeti. Or you can stick a fullback to the goal-post crossbar by the top of his helmet, if that's more to your taste. Mucilage won't do either of these jobs for you. Nor will it

allow you to build a house without using a nail, or mend your cracked Michelangelo. But in its thoroughly unpretentious way, mucilage acts as a well-behaved glue ought to.

First of all, you don't have to worry that it doesn't look gluish. It's neither milk pale nor insubstantially transparent, but that fairly unappetizing yellowish brown that puts you in mind of the ultimate fate of most of the horses you've ever bet on. Second, the word mucilage *sounds* sticky in a believable, human sort of way, not like something that will cement molecules for all eternity.

But best of all, the mucilage bottle comes complete with its own tongue, a wonderful rubber spreader that licks a nice straight line of glue onto the paper (or whatever) and eventually gets so gunked up with dried leavings that you have to perform surgery with a straightened-out paper clip. Reclaiming a mucilage top from the ravages of dry skin is inexpressibly satisfying, and doing the job can take ten minutes away from your real work, which alone is worth the price of a bottle.

Tupperware Containers

To assume that Tupperware is nothing more than a type of plastic container is to underestimate the fervor of that Dionysian revel known as the Tupperware party. There is purity here, a forthright beauty that is grail-like. How else to explain that 150 million pieces of Tupperware are sold every year in thirty-

satin basic container set that can hold its own with any bridal pattern at Tiffany's? Or when he conceived and patented a foolproof snap-on top by inverting the structure of a paint can lid? Probably not. But if his name on the lips of millions of true believers counts for anything at all, beatification seems certain for St. Earl, knight errant of Our Lady of the Leftover.

seven countries? Can Earl S. Tupper have known that he was liable to become the first polymer-age saint when, as a chemist at Du Pont in the late forties, he decided that the polyethylene he had helped develop would be the perfect material for refrigerator storage? Or when he designed the classic white

El Bubble Bubblegum Cigar

What this country needs is a good ten-cent cigar that doesn't smoke up the place, doesn't scatter ashes, and doesn't look awful in an ashtray. Happily, through the intervention of Providence and the Philadelphia Chewing Gum Company, there is El Bubble, which is all these things and more. ☐ Like most great

inventions, the bubblegum cigar was the result of need, economic and technological conditions, logic, and serendipity. When wartime sugar rationing was discontinued in the late forties, the strategic marketers in Philadelphia were quick to conceive the idea of a larger, more expensive kind of chew. (Until then, gum generally sold for a penny and came in slivers so thin that to keep the pleasure alive you had to continually add another piece to your cud.)

As manufacturers of bubblegum cigarettes, a cigar was a natural move for P.C.G.Co.; but since no machine existed capable of extruding a piece of gum with the imposing dimensions of the El Bubble, the company constructed their own and in no time dominated a market that they had invented. The cigar, originally colored a realistic but unpalatable brown, cost a nickel and gave the littlest kid on the block all the cocky swagger of Edward G. Robinson, see? The brain trust at Philadelphia Chewing Gum had more ideas, too. They broke the color barrier by eliminating the light sugar dusting commonly found on gum, which allowed them to produce cigars in unearthly hues of green and blue. But the *coup de théâtre* was the introduction in 1981 of separately boxed "It's a Boy!" and "It's a Girl!" cigars in, of course, blue or pink. Truly, El Bubble is a cigar of another color.

Dom Perignon Champagne

It is unreliably reported that Dom Perignon, the blind monk who in the seventeenth century discovered a vat of wine that had gone off a bit and was consequently effervescent, exclaimed on his first taste of the stuff, "I am drinking the stars!" Just as likely, it seems, is that the good dom, realizing that he had let a

good barrel spoil, drank up the evidence of his malfeasance and, on awaking the next day, cried, "Oy, 'sblood, Mother of Mercy, am I seeing stars!" Whichever, the effect was notable enough for the brothers of the Benedictine Abbey in Hautvillers, France, to try the happy miscalculation again, and again, and aren't we all glad they did!

Dom Perignon (the wine) is a vintage champagne produced from the oldest, most aristocratic

Chardonnay and Pinot Noir vines in the vineyards of Moët and Chandon. It was first blended early in the century for the personal use of the Moët and Chandon families. In 1921 the first *cuvée* was made available to the public, not in France (for some perverse reason) but in the United States. (Not until 1949 could the French buy their own best champagne.) Dom Perignon is made only on those years when the *chef des caves* at Moët deems the best grapes are good enough. In the sixty-two years since it was first introduced, there have been only twenty Dom Perignon vintages produced. Since it ages six years or more and can only be stored for another ten or so, there's never all that much around. The high-quality old vines produce just so many grapes, those grapes produce just so much Dom Perignon, and there are *so many* celebrities.

The Checker Cab: In Memoriam

After seven decades of unquestioned sovereignty, the automobile has at last been reduced from mythic proportions to mere transportation. Its place in our dreams of glory, however, has not diminished. Somewhere, deep within, we still believe in the car as Phaeton, a marvelous chariot that can

give us the speed of the wind and can make us gods three times over (and with four speeds forward). As we squeeze dutifully into little machines with humble, domesticated names like Civic, Omni, and Champ, though we may know that we're doing the responsible thing, there is a void in our souls.

The looming, heroic Lasalles, Deusenbergs, and Packards of the past are long gone. Cadillacs have shrunk so alarmingly that the diminutive "Caddy," never really appropriate before, fits all too well now. Even the Rolls-Royce has traded in its legendary arrogance for the semianonymity of good gray corporate efficiency (lending who knows how many flamboyant sheiks the steady image of a north country tycoon). Until recently, only the Checker still retained the commodiousness of interior and dignified coachwork befitting our lost dreams of the dream machine. And now it, too, is gone.

Designed in the late forties, possibly to answer the question "If there'd been taxis on Mt. Olympus, what would they have been like?" the Checker has changed only slightly over the years (mostly at the meter). The Marathon, a civilian version, has for a long while been the only limo one could enter without doffing one's top hat. Monumental, squared off, plump, and benevolent, the dowager duchess of Kalamazoo has always lived up to its manufacturer's description: "Regally simple, of classical dimensions . . ."

But alas, in a world that is going to the Rabbits, the Checker has been doomed by—of all things—bad gas mileage. And so, a sad adieu to le Checker. For the sake of a few miles per gallon, we are forced to watch the slow extinction of the yellow elephant, one of the great comfortable creatures of our dwindling creature comforts. Yet who knows? Maybe if we all say together "We believe in quintessence," the Checker will come back to life. After all, we saved Tinkerbell that way.